Advance Praise for
THE DEATH GAME

"Dynamite! I am familiar with every one of these cases, which *The Death Game* brings back so vividly. They remind me of when I filed my own *habeas corpus* appeal in 1985. In that year, there were 8,500 similar appeals filed. I was one of the lucky 3% that succeeded. Then, as this book shows, they closed it down even further. I am so thankful that I do not have to rely on today's criminal justice system. Mike Gray has done a great piece of work."

—Rubin "Hurricane" Carter

"A sobering, timely and eloquent look at capital punishment, the American way of death."

—Daniel Schorr
Senior News Analyst
National Public Radio
(for identification only)

"An eye for an eye—even if it's the wrong eye? This great book demonstrates undeniably that during the prosecution of capital cases, plenty of *new* crimes occur. There's lying, cheating, and manufacturing of evidence—by police, witnesses, prosecutors, judges, press, victims and even defense attorneys. All this to arrive at that panacea called "closure." Gray reveals our death penalty as an institution to be a mockery of justice. That mockery taints even the Supreme Court, where Justice Scalia makes clear that proof of innocence doesn't prevent punishment. If you believe in the death penalty, read this book."

—Ed Asner

"Gripping, real-life stories."

—Former U.S. Senator Paul Simon

"A tough and eloquent indictment of the fatal flaws in the death penalty. Mike Gray effectively presents case after case showing how evidence manipulation, incompetent defense counsel and witness fallibility can lead to an unjust death sentence. At a time when calls for a death penalty moratorium are reaching all-time highs, *The Death Game* should be on the desk of every lawmaker, law professor and judge in America."

—John Burton, State Senator, California

"Relentless, ruthless, fearless. To the investigator in Mike Gray, truth is gold. With pan and pick, he's a prospector, ever on the hunt. Driven by the knowledge that what he seeks lies deep beneath the surface, hidden by layers of legalism and rocks of righteousness, he digs away. Gray tunnels unerringly toward the vein of fact that, when freed, enlightens all. With *The Death Game*, he once again emerges, soiled by the process, to strip the mask of respectability from the ceremony of state killing and expose, to our embarrassment, the rot at its core."

—Mike Farrell
actor/writer/producer
and President of Death Penalty Focus

"A trenchant exposé of the political distortions of our justice system."

—from the introduction by
Rudolph J. Gerber
Judge, Arizona Court of Appeals (ret.)
and a former architect of Arizona's death penalty

The Death Game

Capital Punishment and the Luck of the Draw

Mike Gray

Common Courage Press   Monroe, Maine

Copyright © 2003 by Mike Gray
All rights reserved.

Cover design by Matt Wuerker and Erica Bjerning

ISBN 1-56751-191-0 trade hardcover

**Library of Congress Cataloging-in-Publication Data
is available on request from the publisher**

First Printing

Common Courage Press
Box 702
Monroe, ME 04951

(207) 525-0900; FAX (207) 525-3068
orders-info@commoncouragepress.com

See our website for e versions of this book.
www.commoncouragepress.com

Printed in Canada

Dedication

For Mary Brigid Kenney, an honest prosecutor who thought the truth was more important than the job, and for Detective John Sam who refused to make up the facts to fit the program, and for the thousands of other unsung heroes who try day in and day out to save the system from self destruction.

Contents

Introduction

"A Death Penalty We Can Live With"?

Rudolph J. Gerber

I read Mike Gray's trenchant exposé of the political distortions of our justice system from what can only be described as a unique vantage point: I was an architect of Arizona's death penalty. Later, I sat as a judge on the Arizona Court of Appeals.

In the early 1970s, I was a newly-minted lawyer, charged with re-writing Arizona's criminal code, and I drafted major parts of the capital punishment legislation. As we were writing these provisions back in 1973, Senator Sandra Day O'Connor was serving in the Arizona legislature, well before her elevation to the Supreme Court. I asked her what kind of death penalty to draft. She responded without irony or humor by telling me to "draft a death penalty we can live with."

The provisions I drafted were later struck down by the United States Supreme Court in its June, 2002 decision in *Ring v. Arizona*. In its ruling, the Supreme Court found, contrary to the Arizona statutes, that the nation's constitution requires that it must be a jury, rather than a judge, that finds the aggravating factors qualifying a defendant for the death penalty.

After thinking we had succeeded in that effort, I went on in the late 1970s to become a trial judge regularly confronted by zealous prosecutors seeking capital punishment.

My doubts began to surface about the propriety of such sentences. In the final twelve years of my service on the Arizona Court of Appeals they increased. These doubts did not concern the *Ring* issue—whether judges or juries should perform death sentencing. Rather, they were about whether Arizona's death penalty, which I had helped draft and was then sworn to uphold, deserved to survive in the face of evolving moral standards and social science research pointing in an opposite direction.

My judicial robes too long encumbered me from walking that walk. But no longer.

A veteran investigator and commentator on America's criminal justice system, Mike Gray again brings his probing "you are there" style of journalism to bear on our nation's embarrassing devotion to the death penalty. *The Death Game: Capital Punishment and the Luck of the Draw* exposes the triumph of political image over justice in Texas, Illinois, Oklahoma and other jurisdictions. Local prosecutors, police and judges have shamelessly put personal images of toughness above considerations of innocence, to the point of manufacturing evidence and promoting convictions of innocent people. In these pages we read how, in some highly publicized cases like that of Randall Dale Adams, police hide exonerating witnesses; how prosecutors with their eyes on higher office ignore evidence suggesting innocence; how some corrupt judges in Illinois and Texas sacrifice innocent lives in order to further their careers by cultivating an image of toughness at all costs. We also learn how the investigative skills of lawyers and judges pale by comparison to those of Northwestern University journalism students: on a courthouse class assignment, they did the spade work showing the innocence of at least four inmates sentenced to die.

As Governor George Ryan's clemency decisions cleared

the Illinois death row in January, 2003, his critical comments about the broken criminal justice system highlighted exactly what Mike Gray illustrates: the pervasive subordination of defendants' innocence to the political goals of police officers and elected prosecutors and judges.

As Mike Gray observes, Texas may be the nation's most prolific executioner. But Arizona's death sentences per 1,000 homicides—a more accurate measure of the willingness to confer that sentence—exceed those in Texas and other states. Pima County (Tucson) is the nation's per capita leader in seeking and imposing death. Maricopa County (Phoenix) trails it only by a few. Arizona's leading role in per capita death sentencing reflects not so much the law of the old west as politicians' all-too-typical vote pandering by nurturing an image of being tough. It is a trait that serves political advancement. But it is wholly unrelated to being smart or to carrying out justice.

As Gray suggests, a connection exists between zeal for capital punishment and reversible error. As Jim Liebman of Columbia University has also shown, more frequent death sentences correlate with higher court reversals that eventually diminish rather than increase the number of actual executions. In the United States generally, only 5% of the condemned are actually executed. This is a small return, if it can be called that, on such an enormous investment of energy, money and political rhetoric. One reason for that low return is that nationwide about 7 in 10 death sentences are set aside on appeal for trial court errors. In the manufacturing world, a product that had to be recalled 7 of 10 times would not survive in the marketplace. One that "worked" only 5% of the time would lose its following and eventually disappear.

Some of those who wait on our nation's death rows have been found to be factually innocent. Gray tells the stories of

Randall Adams in Texas and Anthony Porter in Illinois, whose factual innocence only began to be discovered as they were approaching their last meals. As of the end of 2002, some 112 persons have been released from our nation's death rows because discoveries of DNA, accurate witness testimony, or the true killers showed that the convicted could not possibly have committed the murders which prompted their death sentences.

Since such sentencing resumed in 1973, the release rate of innocents approximates 1.5% of the total death sentences. In other contexts, such as a pharmacy's sale of a drug that resulted in fatalities, an error rate of 1.5% would cause removal of the offending product and expose the manufacturer and seller to the prospect of punitive damages. Not so with our death penalty.

This high rate of capital error has prompted the governors of Illinois and Maryland to declare moratoriums on executions in their states because of the high risk of executing innocent persons. Some prosecutors and judges, notably in Texas and Illinois, have been all too willing to continue to run that risk. They claim that even an error-prone system addresses the big questions about capital punishment: Does it deter? Does it offer retribution? Does it provide closure? Is it cost effective?

As Gray points out, the answers to these questions are negative. The deterrence claim is one of the most popular for death advocates. More than once President Bush has supported capital punishment by claiming that it "saves lives". Research repeatedly shows otherwise. Sociologists Thorsten Sellin, Michael Radelet and William Bailey have compared execution and homicide rates among similar contiguous states and within the same state during abolition and retention periods. They have found that the presence of a death penalty does not impact homicide rates at all. Those rates are highest in southern states that execute most frequently and lowest in north central states that either execute sparingly or not at all. Nationally, as Gray observes, homicide rates are from 46% to 101% higher in the 38 executing states than in the 12 non-executing states. Even apart from this statistical approach, if deterrence is to work at all, capital punishment would need to be swift and certain. Even here the prospect of deterrence fails because those traits disappear in a system involving an average of 13 years wait for the eventual execution of only 5% of the death row population.

As to retribution—the "eye for an eye" argument espoused in the Bible and also by Thomas Jefferson—the American criminal justice system has simply never embraced the notion of "like deserves like". It does not anywhere rape the rapist, steal from the thief, or pummel the assaulter. In the "death for death" rationale, retribution also fails because 95% of killers who are sentenced to death escape execution. Even in our rare consummated executions we no longer pretend to mimic the brutality of the original killing. Indeed, the evolution of our country's execution liturgy shows a steady progression away from the brutality, publicity and sermonizing of colonial town square hangings. It has moved increasingly to the quiet and painless antiseptics of the closed door lethal injection, a procedure so un-brutal that President Reagan comforted us with the assurance of it being "just like falling asleep". Perhaps such a painless liturgy has become more important for the American public than for the condemned person. In any event, our execution trends show that our justice system somehow realizes that executions involving re-enacting the offender's killing undermine what a justice system professes to teach.

The closure argument, the understandable need of the

victims' surviving family and friends for closure and finality is also popular. It has been invoked more than once by President Bush and Attorney General Ashcroft, notably at the execution of Timothy McVeigh. But it is hardly furthered by a system that executes only 5% of those sentenced to death while frustrating death-expectant victims the other 95% of the time. Nor is closure furthered by a system that takes the victims' survivors on a protracted legal roller coaster of raised and lowered expectations over an average of 13 years before that infrequent execution actually occurs. Such a small return over such a long up-and-down legal labyrinth suggests exactly the opposite of closure and finality.

Then there is the argument on the cost benefits of death. But contrary to the intuitive assumption that execution saves on the costs of incarceration, the costs of an execution exceed those for life imprisonment. Research, notably in California, Texas and Florida—all high-volume executioners—repeatedly shows that the costs of execution outweigh life imprisonment by a factor of three or four to one. Sometimes executions average over $2 million in publicized cases, compared to the much less expensive life imprisonment. The added expense is mostly due to prolonged appeals, reversals, remands, retrials and re-investigations. In mid-August 2002, an Ohio trial judge prohibited the prosecution from seeking a death penalty precisely for reasons of its excessive cost to the county treasury.

As Gray also correctly observes, significant social science research in Arizona, California, Oklahoma and New York finds a "brutalization" effect of some executions on those states' homicide rates. In these and some other states, highly publicized executions have prompted some marginal persons to imitate government conduct by killing when otherwise they would not have done so. In Arizona, as in

Oklahoma, the homicide rate especially involving stranger killings has jumped sharply following the most highly publicized executions. As these pages point out, California murders increased by some 9% in the three months following the highly publicized 1994 execution of Robert Harris. Though the brutalization thesis awaits more research, its developing data at least suggest that the government's execution action might well offer some troubled persons permission to follow that example.

As Gray's investigation shows, our politicians frequently respond to these kinds of attacks with self-serving political narcissism. These are expressed typically via paeans about the need for justice and being tough on crime and ululations about the plight of victims. When Diane Feinstein served on the California Parole Board, she opposed the death penalty; when she ran for Congress from that state, she became an ardent death penalty advocate, though she was never able to provide her promised research supporting her deterrence claims. As a leading black spokesman, Andrew Young opposed the death penalty; when he ran for governor of Georgia, he became pro-death because, in his view, police morale needed executions. (Texas, the state that has the highest volume of executions, also has the highest volume of police killings.) When William Weld ran for governor of Massachusetts, he claimed that the death penalty's deterrent effect inherently exceeded all social science research; it could only be intuited "in one's gut." Senator Bob Graham of Florida has echoed similar mystical claims about this elusive, immeasurable statistic hiding behind all empirical evaluation.

These contradictions in the very name of our "justice" system appear in Gray's exposés of how some states' politicians put justice and innocence secondary to personal image. The unstated conclusion to this book is probably obvious:

our death system is collapsing under the weight of its reversals, its demagoguery, and its false pretenses. We need to take a look at how the rest of the civilized world treats death. If we did, we might well answer Justice O'Connor's mandate of 30 years ago differently: there is no death penalty we can live with while we play such "games."

—Rudolph J. Gerber
Judge, Arizona Court of Appeals (ret.),
School of Justice Studies,
Arizona State University
January 15, 2003

Foreword

Daniel Gaul

In November 2000, I was confronted with one of the most critical decisions that anyone could ever face: Do I spare a guilty defendant or condemn him to die? As a judge presiding over one of the busiest trial courts in America, this decision fell to me when a jury recommended the death penalty for a defendant convicted of shooting and killing a Cleveland police officer.

As the patrolman looked at the defendant's driver's license, the defendant shot the officer in the face at point blank range. The defendant testified and admitted the shooting, claiming no defense other than that of a reflexive action.

With the airtight evidence and the compelling nature of the case, the jury reached a quick and predictable verdict. Applying Ohio's court-tested death penalty statute, the jury recommended death. It was up to me to accept their recommendation or sentence the defendant to life imprisonment without the possibility of parole.

Then and now, my underlying belief is that the death penalty simply does not work. The question of morality aside, I believe the death penalty accomplishes nothing. It serves neither as a deterrent, a cost-effective punishment, nor a method of providing closure to victims' families or the community.

I am increasingly concerned with the arbitrary, reckless, and some would say malicious, pursuit of the death penalty by prosecutors immune from civil and criminal liability. But most importantly, increased scrutiny of death sentences and the emerging technology of DNA analysis were demonstrating that many innocent people have been wrongly sentenced to death. I have seen these problems first hand: once, because of prosecutorial misconduct, I had to reverse a murder conviction.

Now, with this guilty defendant before me, my choice was stark: Would I fulfill my sworn duty, follow the law and, as the statute clearly requires, impose the death sentence? Or would I interject my personal beliefs to save him?

In a packed courtroom on Thursday, November 16, 2000, I made the difficult decision. I sentenced the defendant to death. Then, after stepping down from the bench and removing my robe, a conscious gesture designed to contrast my role of judge with my right as a private citizen, I forcefully denounced the death penalty in front of the media gathered at an impromptu press conference.

Ultimately my sense of duty, the sworn "duty to uphold the laws of the State of Ohio," proved my primary consideration. I thought it inappropriate to cast aside the rule of law to implement my personal beliefs — even to spare the defendant's life. However, as the individual charged with the burden of handing down the death sentence, I felt morally compelled to utilize the moment to point out the abject failure of capital punishment in America.

I have been a vigorous opponent of the death penalty ever since.

My record makes me either the best or the worst spokesperson against the death penalty. I'll let you decide. My experience "tinkering with the machinery of death"—in the words of late U.S. Supreme Court Justice Harry Blackmun—is eerily similar to the lethal distinction courts all over the country have made for the last 30 years.

In 1972, the U.S. Supreme Court struck down the death penalty, ruling it was cruel and unusual as it was then arbitrarily applied. The Court's action thereby voided all states' death penalty laws. Since then the issue of capital punishment has weighed heavily on the collective conscience of the nation, triggering an intense national debate. Now re-instated in 38 states and propelled by constant court challenges, the death penalty has become undoubtedly one of the most divisive social issues of our time.

On January 11 of this year, the debate reached an even higher crescendo when Illinois Governor George Ryan commuted the death sentences of all 164 inmates on the state's death row. A Republican, Ryan issued this blanket commutation after instituting a moratorium on all executions in January 2000. During the moratorium Ryan pardoned 17 death row inmates. All pardons were granted on the basis of actual innocence. Some inmates were spared just hours before impending execution.

Ryan's decision occurred after his office performed a three-year examination of Illinois' death penalty that exposed the "catastrophic failure" of the system. Describing the current law as "arbitrary and capricious and therefore immoral," Ryan criticized the system as "an absolute embarrassment."

Reaction to Ryan's decision ranged from ecstasy to outrage, and special interest groups on different sides of the issue held the governor in both adoration and contempt. Agree or disagree, most understand that the experience in Illinois symbolizes the intense and often destructive depth of feeling associated with the issue of capital punishment in America.

Mike Gray's *The Death Game: Capital Punishment and the Luck of the Draw* is of great assistance in understanding the complexities of the issue. His critique is devastating. From Texas to Illinois, Georgia to California, Gray reveals a haphazard system replete with pervasive racism, corruption and incompetence. In gripping narrative, he exposes the death penalty for the counterproductive, ineffective and morally bereft system that it is, particularly in light of alternative punishments such as life imprisonment without the possibility of parole.

The Death Game was a book I couldn't put down, but at times I couldn't bear to read. Gray pierces the protective shroud of the criminal justice system and reminds us, in stark and staggering imagery, of the many innocent lives taken, and of those almost taken, at the hands of our government. And his book serves as notice that the problems inherent in the death penalty are national in scope. Injustice doesn't stop at any particular state line.

Nationally, the number of human beings who have been released from death row because they were innocent has surpassed 100. Their releases were not because of legal sleight of hand, but because of their innocence. This fact alone should provide any fair-minded American with the moral clarity necessary to oppose capital punishment.

—Daniel Gaul
Judge
Cleveland Court of Common Pleas
Cleveland, Ohio
January 22, 2003

CHAPTER ONE

"You have the right to remain silent. Anything you say can and will be used against you in a court of law. You have the right to an attorney. If you cannot afford an attorney, one will be appointed for you without charge."[1]

—U.S. Supreme Court

HOUSTON—MAY 13, 1981—9:35 P.M.

Bernadine Skillern screams through the windshield at the man with the gun—"Don't! Don't! Don't!"

Right in front of her under the glare of lights in the Safeway parking lot a white man with a bag of groceries is getting mugged. A black teenager has a gun to his head. In a flash of amazing courage Bernadine leans on her horn and screams at the kid. He glances at her for a heart-stopping second. Then he turns back to his victim. "POP!"

The white guy drops his groceries and collapses on the hood of a parked car as the shooter dashes for the street. At this point, everybody within range hits the deck. But not Bernadine Skillern. She drops into gear and peels out after him, almost cutting him off at the exit. Framed in her headlights, he looks directly at her again—probably wondering if he's run into the Lone Ranger.

But Bernadine isn't alone. She has two kids in the car with her and they're screaming their lungs out for mommy to stop. She's done all she can. She slams on the brakes and the black kid disappears into the night. The victim, mortally wounded, staggers into the Safeway and hits the floor face down.

In minutes the Houston Police are all over the place

and when the detectives get to Bernadine Skillern she's positive she can identify the killer. She got a good look at him over a period of sixty to ninety seconds, mostly from the back and side, but for few seconds he looked directly at her. It was unforgettable.[2]

The police couldn't have asked for a better eyewitness. Black, middle-class, reputable, Ms. Skillern is an elementary school secretary. Her description is precise. The image of the killer in the headlights is burned into her mind—short hair, light complexion, thin face, no facial hair. He was wearing a white coat.

Seven days later the Houston Police have a kid in custody who matches the description, a vicious seventeen-year-old street punk named Gary Graham who's been on a violent rampage in the week since the murder. They've connected him to twenty armed robberies—five last Friday alone—and there's no doubt he's capable of killing. He shot and wounded three of his robbery victims.[3]

In a state where the murder rate can sometimes outpace car accidents as a cause of death, there is nothing to suggest that this savage killing is anything out of the ordinary. None of the players have any reason to believe that they are involved in a case that will one day split the highest court in the land by one vote just minutes before a scheduled execution.

HOUSTON—MAY 21, 1981

At the police station the detectives lay out an array of five mug shots for Ms. Skillern. And since even the best eyewitnesses can make mistakes, the cop who selected the pictures apparently decides to give Bernadine a little help. Of the five photographs, only one matches her description—

short hair, thin face, clean shaven. The other four are markedly different—bushy Afros, moustaches or beards, full faces.

Skillern, not surprisingly, zeroes in on the only short-haired slender face on the table—Gary Graham. "That looks the most like him." But she says the man she saw had a darker complexion. And his face was thinner.[4]

The next day Bernadine Skillern is shown a lineup at headquarters. Once again there seems to be an effort to minimize the possibility of a mistake on her part. Of the five men she saw in the mug shots, only one is in the police lineup—Graham. She spots him and begins trembling. She doesn't realize that the window she's looking through is a one-way mirror. She thinks he can see her. The detective escorts her into the hallway. She tells him she's positive it's the man in the number three position.[5]

Case closed. It's a perfectly logical fit. The Safeway murder was committed on Wednesday, May 13th, 1981, and for the next six days this young scumbag was ripping Houston apart—rape, robbery, car jacking—leaving several people in the hospital. Whatever triggered this explosion, it obviously began with the murder in the Safeway parking lot.

But there is a cautionary note. As one of the officers is driving her home, Bernadine Skillern talks about what just happened. She says she recognized Gary Graham in the lineup as the man "in the photo."[6] That means there's a possibility she picked Graham out of the lineup, not because of his resemblance to the killer, but because she saw his mug shot last night—a mug shot she said then only "looks most like him."

HOUSTON—OCTOBER 1981

If Attorney Ron Mock had known about this highly suggestive identification process he might not have done anything about it anyway. Three years out of law school with a dismal academic record and a serious interest in demon rum, Mock has a reputation for go-along affability and general laziness. He boasts about the fact that he flunked criminal law at Texas Southern.[7] With these qualifications, he has become an essential cog in the Harris County criminal justice system of the 1980s. There is no official public defender here, so the choice of a defense attorney is up to the judge. And since it's in everybody's interest to keep things moving, a lawyer like Ron Mock can be counted on to fulfill the legal requirements without throwing sand in the gears. The pay isn't that great but Mock is able to make up for it in volume. As one of the few black defense attorneys available for this kind of work, he's grossing $150,000 a year. He has a Rolls, a Harley, and a piece of the action in several downtown saloons.[8]

When Mock looks over the state's evidence against Gary Graham he finds it overwhelming. Considering the twenty armed robberies the kid committed in the week after the murder, Mock feels his biggest problem will be to keep the jury from finding out about this one-man crime wave. He decides it's best not to provoke the prosecutors. Mock calls no witnesses of his own during the trial and doesn't bother to cross-examine the state's witnesses either. He offers no evidence at all, and when confronted with the laser-like certainty of Bernadine Skillern's identification, he doesn't delve into the details of how she came to select Graham from the lineup. Instead he tells the jury that Bernadine Skillern should get a standing ovation for bravery.[9] While that's certainly true—few of us would have the guts to do what she did—it proves to be a losing strategy for his client. The trial is wrapped up in two days and, with no challenge to Skillern's identification, the verdict is a forgone conclusion. After deliberating for a matter of hours, the jury convicts Gary Graham of murder in the first degree. The penalty phase is even quicker. Mock calls only two witnesses to speak on Graham's behalf. Again the jury is back in a flash and the verdict is death.

HOUSTON—FEBRUARY, 1993

By the time Dick Burr gets involved in the Gary Graham case it has already reached the U.S. Supreme Court. Burr, a square-jawed civil rights attorney from Lake Wales, Florida, is with the NAACP Legal Defense Fund out of New York. As head of the Death Penalty Project, he's one of the country's leading experts on capital punishment and he's been brought on board for added firepower.

Graham's lead counsel, Mandy Welch, is a bright young lawyer from rural Oklahoma with a growing reputation in the select club of death penalty specialists. She is head of the Texas Resource Center in Houston, a federally-funded office that Congress set up to aid the defenseless. She and Burr hit it off immediately, and it's a good thing. The Gary Graham case is about to engulf them both.

In the late 1980s, before these two picked up the reins, Graham was represented by an attorney named Doug O'Brien. Every Texas death penalty case gets one automatic appellate review and O'Brien volunteered to handle it. After digging through the evidence, he became convinced that Graham had been railroaded. When the appeal was denied, he was so distressed he stayed on the case for free. Without funds, his investigation had to be limited to the information at his fingertips, but he hit pay dirt without getting out of his chair.

Even a casual reading of the trial transcript suggests that Ron Mock had done little more than grease the skids for the prosecution. Among other things, there were several alibi witnesses who claimed they were with Graham on the night of the murder. During the original trial they had approached Ron Mock and offered to testify but he had brushed them off. So in July of 1987, O'Brien filed a petition in state court for a new trial, cataloguing Mock's courtroom failings, including his refusal to call these alibi witnesses to the stand.

Graham's case was then in the hands of state judge Donald Shipley, and in February of 1988 Shipley listened to three of these alibi witnesses testify under oath, then ruled that they weren't credible because they were related to the defendant.

Doug O'Brien immediately filed for relief in federal court, where the case bounced around like a ping-pong ball for the next five years. What kept it in midair was the issue of "youthfulness." Graham was seventeen at the time of the murder and a national debate was then raging about where to draw the line. Should we be executing people who can't legally drink or vote or see an X-rated movie? Graham, on the other hand, was practically a poster boy for the death penalty—a savage young marauder who had gunned down Bobby Lambert, a defenseless white man with a bag of groceries. In spite of this handicap, O'Brien actually got the federal appellate court to call for a new sentencing trial, leaving the conviction intact but allowing a second look at the death sentence. Then the State of Texas appealed and the federal court reversed itself.

Despite Dick Burr's assistance, the U.S. Supreme Court finally decided they couldn't touch the case for technical reasons. If they agreed that Graham's death sentence was unconstitutional because of his age, it would represent a "new rule of law." But a new rule of law that comes from a proceeding like this can't be applied retroactively—the court is unequivocal about that—so even a favorable decision wouldn't help Graham.

HOUSTON—MARCH, 1993

Gary Graham's date with death is set for April 29. But Dick Burr is now on the case full time. Mandy Welch has talked him into taking over as lead counsel and there are few people in the country with his expertise in this business. Since Welch's Texas Resource Center has access to cash, Burr's first move is to do the investigation that Ron Mock should have done 12 years ago.

The initial surprise is right there in the transcript. On careful reading, Burr notices that the jury was asked to leave the courtroom just before Bernadine Skillern testified. The judge then held a brief discussion about her testimony, and one line from this dialogue jumps out at Burr. With the jury out of the room, the police officer on the witness stand makes a stunning admission. It seems that the night Bernadine Skillern picked Gary Graham out of the lineup, there was another eyewitness present. His name was Ron Hubbard and his reaction to the lineup was quite different. He told the police that Gary Graham was not the shooter.

It's been a dozen years since the trial but Ron Hubbard is easy enough to locate. He's a veteran postal service employee now and he's more than willing to talk. What he has to say gives Burr a jolt. On that fatal night in May of

1981, Hubbard was a box-boy at the Safeway market and he remembers the man in the white coat. He walked right past the guy. Hubbard was out in the lot collecting shopping carts shortly before the shooting and he saw this man leaning against one of the columns. He passed directly in front of him, spoke to him, looked him in the eye. This man, says Hubbard, didn't look anything like Gary Graham. And he wasn't nearly as tall. At 5'-10", Hubbard is the same height as Gary Graham. This other guy was about half-a-foot shorter.

Burr and Welch try to talk to Bernadine Skillern—she declines—but there were a couple of other people in the parking lot that night who did testify at the trial. One is dead of a heart attack but Burr finds the other, a woman named Wilma Amos. Ms. Amos was loading groceries in her van that night when the shooter ran past. She's 5'-2" and she says the gunman was about her size—maybe 5'-3" or 5'-4"—no taller than that. She didn't think it was Gary Graham then or now.

Burr's team also finds a 12-year-old kid who was there. Leodis Wilkerson, sitting in his father's car, had seen it all go down. Now 24, Leodis still remembers the scene and one thing sticks in his mind. The shooter was shorter than the victim. The victim was 5'-6". Graham is four inches taller.

Burr is amazed. They've already found three eyewitnesses who say Graham was not the man, and they haven't even been able to see the police report yet. "The D.A.'s office refuses to give it to us," says Burr. But with Graham's execution date just ten days away, they've got to move.

On April 20, 1993, Burr files a petition asking the state court to let these new witnesses testify under oath. Six days later they're called to appear before Judge Shipley. Then, an hour before their court appearance, Burr gets word that the D.A. has finally turned over the police report.

At a glance, it's explosive. It seems there were several other witnesses in addition to the ones they've just discovered and one of them got an even better look at the shooter than Ron Hubbard. The police report also raises serious questions about the identification process that Bernadine Skillern went through. Burr heads for the courtroom ready to press his argument to the wall.

But Judge Shipley is in the middle of jury selection on another trial. He refuses to hear any argument. He takes a break just long enough to sign an order denying relief. He says these eyewitnesses are not credible because Bernadine Skillern actually saw the man pull the trigger. These other people "did not witness the actual shooting..."Dismissing their descriptions, he says, "the height discrepancies of three to four inches in the height approximations...of the black male they saw running in the parking lot do not discredit Bernadine Skillern's facial identification..."[10]

Burr's client now has less than 72 hours to live. He appeals directly to Governor Ann Richards for a stay. The Governor takes a look at the case and she decides there are too many loose ends. She grants a one-month reprieve, pushing the date back to June 3.

Now Burr and his team fall on the police report with a vengeance and they quickly find what they're looking for— the details of Bernadine Skillern's I.D. of Gary Graham. "After seeing the photo array with Gary in it," says Burr, "Ms. Skillern was drawn to him. But she says 'the person I saw had a darker complexion and a thinner face.'" The report also reveals that after the lineup she said that she'd recognized Gary Graham as the same man she'd seen in the photo the night before. A look at the mug shots she was shown that night reveals that only one was even close to her description of the shooter. This is exactly the kind of subtle guidance—conscious or unconscious—that has proven to lead to eyewitness error in case after case.[11] Dr. Elizabeth Loftus, Past President of the American Psychological Society, is an eyewitness identification authority who specifically criticized the process by which Bernadine Skillern was led to identify Gary Graham.

But the most stunning revelation in the report is the discovery of yet another eyewitness who had a better look at the man in the white coat than anyone. Sherian Etuk, now a Harris Country Child Protective Services employee, was working that night as a cashier at the Safeway. For nearly half an hour she saw the killer standing right outside the window near her checkout counter. He was leaning against the column just as Ron Hubbard described him. For some reason she kept an eye on him between customers. This guy, she says, was about 5'-3" and she had a pretty good gage: she was married to a man who was 5'-3".

As Etuk turned to wait on a customer, she heard a shot. She looked up and saw Bobby Lambert stagger and the man in the white coat making a run for it. When the police arrived she told them she hadn't seen the actual shooting but she had a clear look at the shooter before and after.

If Ron Mock had simply read the police report and called this woman to the stand, there is every likelihood that Gary Graham would not be on death row tonight. But Dick Burr has no time for laments. He has to get these eyewitnesses in front of an impartial judge. The new execution date is 30 days away.

Since Judge Shipley has already slammed the door, Burr takes the case to the Texas Court of Criminal Appeals. Arguing that he's uncovered a minefield of new information casting doubt on Graham's guilt, Burr asks the court to reopen the case and force Judge Shipley to hear all these witnesses under oath. The appellate court says no. They tell Burr that if he wants to pursue this line, he'll have to start all over again and file a new petition. On the other hand, they're willing to grant a brief stay of execution. Graham's date with the needle is pushed back to August 16.

At this point, Burr and his team have had enough of Texas justice. "The state courts have been extremely hostile," he says. It's time to move to the federal courts. Once again, they've got less than a month.

On July 22, 1993, Burr files the petition with the U.S. District Court for the Southern District of Texas, followed by a flurry of motions arguing that the state process was unfair. All Judge Shipley did, says Burr, was to blindly sign the order proposed by the state. How can you rule that the new witnesses are not credible without hearing them? Burr also wants to dig further into the prosecution's files. "We think there is more information that's not in the police report."

Over the next three weeks, Burr and his team make repeated requests to appear before the U.S. District Court to argue their motion. They hear nothing. Then three days before the execution they get a fax from the judge denying relief and denying a stay. The federal courts must defer to the state courts, he says.

Fortunately for Gary Graham, his lawyers always seem to have another rabbit in the hat. A lawsuit—*Graham* v. *Texas Board of Pardons and Paroles*—has been filed in civil court charging that the state's clemency process is fundamentally flawed because it provides no fact-finding procedure for people who might actually be innocent. Taken by surprise—civil courts aren't supposed to be involved in criminal matters—the judge in the Austin civil case issues a temporary restraining order that says the state can't touch Gary Graham until the question is resolved.

Outflanked and outraged, the state prosecutors immediately ask the Court of Appeals to overturn the restraining order so they can execute Graham as scheduled, but the court decides to deal with all this confusion by granting its own temporary stay of execution. For the third time this year Graham's date with death is set aside.

It is precisely this sort of legalistic maneuvering that drives death penalty proponents like Dianne Clements crazy. A temporary restraining order is normally used for things like stopping a landlord from evicting tenants or preventing the city from chopping down shade trees. No one expected this end run around the criminal justice system and there is outrage in Houston among a growing chorus of citizens who believe Gary Graham has already had his day in court. He's been on death row now for twelve years and his case has already been to the Supreme Court twice. What more does he want?

Dianne Clements knows something about murderers and murder victims. Her young son was shot to death a few years ago and she set out to honor his memory by founding Justice for All, the country's first and largest victims' rights group. She wants to make sure Gary Graham does not cheat the Angel of Death. The Justice for All website charges Burr and his team with "a cynical fraud wherein lies, half-truths and intimidation have come together in an attempt to free the guilty and punish the law abiding... The pro-Graham movement is mounting an assault by death penalty opponents to abolish the death penalty in Texas and throughout the United States. But for most Texans, it is more than that. It is an attack on our safety."

NEW ORLEANS—AUGUST, 1996

The U.S. Court of Appeals for the Fifth Circuit decides that Dick Burr is right. These heretofore ignored eyewitnesses—Ron Hubbard and Sherian Etuk—should be heard in open court where they can be cross-examined and their credibility fairly judged.

It is a moment of triumph for Dick Burr and Mandy Welch, personally as well as professionally. After months of working side by side into the night and living on Pepsi and pizza, they have fallen in love. They were married last year, he for the second time, she for the third, and they have been moving in lockstep ever since.

It's a good thing they have each other to lean on. Although they have prevailed on the main point, the devil is in the details and this time they have been tripped by their own cleverness. Two years ago they filed a civil suit against the State of Texas charging that the 30-day cutoff for claims of innocence violated Graham's rights. That case was just decided in Graham's favor, which means the Texas courts can now consider Graham's petition to hear the new eyewitnesses. Since that opening now exists, the federal judges feel that Burr and Welch have missed a wicket in the legal croquet game. Before they can proceed in federal court, they must first exhaust all possible remedies in the state. If the Texas courts rule against them, then they can come back here.

Burr protests vehemently. He says they've already been through the wringer in Texas and the courts there have completely rejected his arguments. "There is no reason to believe they'll be any less hostile if you send us back this time," he says. "This man is innocent. He deserves a hearing. You agreed. Please send him back to the federal district court for the hearing that he deserves."

The U.S. Fifth Circuit, however, is not famous for bold decisions and the federal judiciary has lately been under constant fire from the states for meddling in death penalty cases. The judges insist that Burr follow formal procedures. They dismiss Graham's case "without prejudice," meaning they'll be ready to hear it, but only after Burr makes another trip through the Texas courts.

At this point, everything grinds to a halt. Early in 1997 Dick Burr finds himself sucked into the vortex of the decade's most infamous killer. At the request of the Federal Defender and the Chief Judge of the U.S. District Court of Western Oklahoma, Burr is asked to defend Oklahoma City bomber Timothy McVeigh in the sentencing phase of his trial. They need someone of Burr's stature to make sure the trial is unassailable. This case, tried in Denver, effectively ties Burr down for the rest of the year in a futile attempt to save McVeigh from the death penalty.

HOUSTON—DECEMBER, 1997

When Burr returns to Houston at the end of the year he contacts Gary Graham on death row and gets back in harness. The first step is to get the permission of the Texas Court of Criminal Appeals to file a new petition, and within ninety days he's ready. In April of 1998 he files the appeal and waits. Seven months pass. Then in November—without hearing arguments from Burr or his colleagues—the Court of Criminal Appeals issues a terse one-paragraph order slamming the door. Graham's execution is now set for January 12, 1999.

Dick Burr is often floored but never flat-footed. Since the Court of Criminal Appeals has refused to hear Graham's plea in Texas, the door is now open to federal court. He immediately refiles the case with the U.S. Fifth Circuit in New Orleans, reminding them that they have already agreed the new Graham witnesses must be heard.

But in the months since the U.S. Fifth Circuit sent Burr back to Texas state court, the dealer has changed the game. A new federal law—the Anti-terrorism and Effective Death Penalty Act—is about to create an inescapable Catch-22 for Gary Graham.

The "AEDPA," as it's known, is a popular piece of tough-on-crime legislation designed to limit the power of federal judges to second-guess the state courts. Signed into law in 1996, it was born of frustration on the part of state prosecutors everywhere who saw clever lawyers like Dick Burr dragging these death penalty cases on forever. Here, for example, was Gary Graham, still breathing fifteen years after he was sentenced to die.

One delaying tactic the legislators intended to do away with was the strategy that defense attorneys use to keep the game going by playing their cards one at a time. If a defendant has, say, four separate reasons to get a new trial, his attorney could file the petitions one after another and get four turns at bat. The AEDPA was specifically targeted at this litigious gamesmanship. The new rule says that if the evidence, whatever it is, could have been presented earlier, it's too late now. You can't bring it up unless it's legitimately new information that could not have been discovered earlier.

The Texas prosecutors insist that the AEDPA has closed the federal door on Gary Graham. Arguing before the Fifth Circuit in New Orleans, they say that he's lost his right to appeal any further because his so-called "new" eyewitnesses, Sherian Etuk and Ron Hubbard, are named in the original police report. That information was available to Ron Mock nineteen years ago. If it was important, Mock should have brought it up in then. He didn't. Now it's too late.

Burr says this argument is outrageous. He says the AEDPA can't be used against Gary Graham because he's already appeared before this court and they've already agreed that these new eyewitnesses must be heard. The Fifth Circuit itself insisted that Burr go back to the state. He did. Now, after the predictable rejection by the Texas legal system, he's back as promised seeking the same thing he's been after for seven years—a chance to put Sherian Etuk and Ron Hubbard under oath in open court. The AEDPA, says Burr, cannot be applied retroactively to a case that was already in progress. He reminds the Fifth Circuit judges that the AEDPA was already on the books when they sent him back to Texas. They agreed then that Burr could bring the case back if Texas turned him down. Surely they didn't intend to lock the door behind him.

But in this business you have to be prepared for anything. It's Sunday, January 11, and Gary Graham's execution is set for 6:00 p.m. tomorrow night. While waiting for the Fifth Circuit to rule, Burr is at his computer in the ramshackle Houston duplex that serves as his office. He's madly pounding out the next set of briefs for the Supreme Court—just in case— when the phone rings. It's the clerk of the Fifth Circuit. He says the court has granted a stay. They've agreed to hear oral arguments.

Burr exhales. "This means they are going to take our argument seriously."

He's even more positive after he makes his case in New Orleans the following month. The three judges on the appellate panel let him go on much longer than expected and they seem seriously engaged. In the courtroom, watching Burr in action, a number of the country's leading death penalty lawyers agree that he hit the ball out of the park.

There is a lone skeptic—Burr's partner, Mandy Welch. She was watching the jurists on the bench and she had a knot in her stomach. But that evening she gets caught up in the celebration along with everybody else. They all agree the argument went very, very well for Graham.

HOUSTON—MARCH 5, 1999

Burr and Welch are in their office when they get the fax. Burr rips it from the machine and scans it in disbelief. He hands it to Mandy. The Fifth Circuit has affirmed the state's position. Under the guidelines of the AEDPA, Gary Graham's appeal is too late.

"You know there's a part of you that always expects that you'll lose when you're in a court system like this," says Burr. "But this feels worse than almost any other loss I've had." The court has simply ignored its previous ruling. "They said we're entitled to a hearing. Then we come back in and they trap us with this hideous opinion that denies everything."

Once again, Graham's fate has been determined by the luck of the draw. There are 13 federal jurisdictions in the country and they don't all agree on this interpretation of the AEDPA. "We have what's called a split among the circuits," says Burr. "There are other federal appellate courts that would agree with us." The Fifth Circuit in New Orleans is not one of them.

Without missing a beat, Burr and his team move to the next trench. In June of 1999 they file a petition with the U.S. Supreme Court asking for a review of the Fifth Circuit's decision. But the anger that propels them is now tempered with fear. They can feel the ground shifting beneath them.

The AEDPA is symptomatic of a broad political push to speed up the death penalty process. The American people are fed up with a system that leaves convicted killers like Graham languishing at taxpayers expense for ten or twenty years. And lawyers like Dick Burr, once seen as heroes of the civil rights movement, are looked upon now as tricksters and charlatans who are out to free the guilty.

Given the climate, Burr decides to hedge his bet by pursuing a brand new line of attack. In the original police investigation, there were some intriguing details about the victim. Bobby Lambert was a 53-year-old private pilot from Tucson, Arizona, who turns out to have been involved in the illegal drug trade. One curious note—the cops found $6000 in cash in his back pocket when he died. He had just moved to Houston and he had several weapons in his van.

Burr then discovers that there were some folks in Oklahoma who did indeed have an interest in Bobby Lambert and it had nothing to do with cash. A few months earlier, Lambert had been nailed by federal agents for "piloting a plane carrying 40,000 Quaaludes and several ounces of cocaine" into an airstrip near Oklahoma City.[12] But the feds were after bigger fish this time. They granted Lambert immunity so they could put him in front of a federal grand jury and force him to testify about the people who hired him. When the grand jury convened, however, Bobby Lambert was unable to testify because he had been shot in the Safeway parking lot a short time earlier.

Burr and his people have been aware of this startling fact for a while now but they've had neither the time nor resources to pursue it. Private eyes are expensive and since Congress has virtually cut off funding for organizations like Mandy Welch's Texas Resource Center, she and Burr are now operating on a shoestring. But after the Fifth Circuit decision, Burr's investigators are as furious as he is. They agree to pursue the Bobby Lambert investigation for free.

With the dawn of the new millennium, however, the remarkable case of Gary Graham takes another unexpected turn. The governor of Texas announces he will run for President on the Republican ticket and suddenly the politics of capital punishment are on the front burner.

AUSTIN—JANUARY, 2000

With 450 prisoners on death row in Texas and over a hundred executions already under his belt, Governor George W. Bush suddenly finds he's become a lightning rod in the death penalty debate. He has already been subjected to considerable heat on the issue and he has stood his ground. In January of 1998 he sent Christian convert Karla Faye Tucker to her death despite direct appeals from conservative allies like the Reverend Pat Robertson. That was 75 executions ago. Governor Bush has made it clear that he will follow the letter of the law. The only factors he will consider are questions of innocence, and whether or not the prisoner has had full access to the courts. But the Governor's political ambitions guarantee that the Gary Graham drama will be played out on the national stage.

Meanwhile, breaking news from the Midwest is beginning to intrude on the death penalty debate. The *Chicago Tribune*, after a two-year investigation, has published a devastating indictment of the death penalty as practiced in Illinois. Reporters Ken Armstrong and Steve Mills have blown the lid off the state's criminal justice system with a series of stories detailing prosecutorial misconduct, planted evidence, perjured testimony, and jailhouse confessions achieved by applying electricity to the suspect's genitals. New evidence, dug up largely by volunteers and college students, has so far freed over a dozen men from death row—one of them within hours of execution. The actual tally in Illinois for the last twenty years is unnerving—12 executed and 13 freed. It raises the ugly possibility that the state has been killing innocent people.[13]

When confronted with these revelations, Governor Bush is unimpressed. Illinois may have problems but Texas does not. "As far as I'm concerned there has not been one innocent person executed since I've been governor."[14]

This is the kind of challenge a professional newsman lives for. The Chicago Tribune reporters are on the next plane south. Over 130 people have received the needle on Bush's watch, and the Tribune investigators decide to dig through every case—transcripts, briefs, witnesses, lawyers, judges, and the disciplinary records of the defense attorneys. They discover a rat's nest of incompetence and malfeasance that makes Illinois justice look positively Olympian.

In 40 out of these 130 capital cases, defense attorneys like Ron Mock more or less sat on their hands throughout the trial, presenting an occasional witness, but generally no evidence whatsoever. In 29 cases, the prosecutors managed to introduce testimony from Dr. James Grigson, a psychiatrist known as "Dr. Death," who claimed the remarkable ability to predict the defendant's future violence without meeting the defendant. This parlor trick got him kicked out of his own professional society. Dr. Grigson was expelled from the American Psychiatric Association in 1995 because of his unfounded speculation about the future actions of defendants he had not bothered to examine. By then he had helped send scores of people to death row, and at $150 an hour it was a pretty lucrative business. His testimony was so much in demand by prosecutors that in the 1980s he was making $150,000 a year on the witness stand.[15]

Among the other witnesses who sent these 130 individuals to oblivion was a forensic scientist on temporary release from a psychiatric ward, and a pathologist who admitted that he faked an occasional autopsy.[16]

In 43 cases, the defense attorneys were later punished, suspended or kicked out of the profession altogether. Twenty-three cases relied on hair samples as evidence, a technique that experts now say is slightly less reliable than flipping a coin. And in another 23 cases, conviction depended on the testimony of jailhouse snitches—criminals who receive substantial and often secret rewards for climbing in bed with the prosecutors.[17]

But when the Tribune series hits the newsstand, Governor Bush sticks to his guns. The truth is, say his spokesmen, the criminal justice system in Texas has improved significantly in the last several years. For example, minimum standards are now required for death penalty defense attorneys. They have to pass a test on death penalty law. Unfortunately, the people sent to death row before 1995 missed out on this enlightened policy. Gary Graham's attorney, Ron Mock, no longer takes death penalty cases because he took the new test and didn't pass it.

HOUSTON—MARCH 21, 2000

Dick Burr sits in his cluttered office surrounded by file boxes and mountains of briefs as he contemplates the prospects. Gary Graham's case has been before the Supreme Court for eight months and he hasn't heard a peep. "There are now seven eyewitnesses who would have exonerated him some way or another. The jury didn't hear any of that."

The nonstop roller-coaster he's been riding for the last several months is taking its toll. He drops to the sofa by the window like a sack of coal. "What we're working on right now is trying to solve the crime. Trying to figure out who did kill this guy. And that's hard to do when you're not the police. We have some suspects but we can't get access to all the records because we don't have subpoena power."

As for Graham's chances in court, he's hopeful, but not very. "I think there is a sense that people who get targeted for prosecution are bad people anyway," he says, "the lowest of the low, the people we need to get rid of. And somehow there is a cleansing effect in getting rid of them. Gary Graham, for example, had pled guilty to ten charges of aggravated robbery and assault. He didn't contest it. But he said, 'I'm innocent of the murder.' Well, who cares? I mean his defense lawyer didn't even investigate. He said, 'I figured he was guilty.'

"So all the people we don't like...people of color, poor people—nameless, faceless, hated people—get to be targets," says Burr. "And once they're targets, there's a sense that whether it's the right person or not is less important. They've become something else. They're symbols."

DEATH ROW—
HUNTSVILLE, TEXAS—APRIL, 2000

Gary Graham is aware of symbolism. If the State of Texas can play this game, so can he. During his two decades in this six-by-twelve cubicle, he has transformed himself from a street punk into a revolutionary and his relentless push for a new trial has taken on the trappings of a crusade.

Graham's charge of racism resonates among the brothers in Houston's Fifth Ward, and it also resonates across the nation. Whatever the merits of this particular case, there is a consensus among African Americans that they are singled out for special treatment and the facts bear them out. In the State of Texas fully a third of the young black males are locked up or under court supervision, and a black kid here is twice as likely to be treated as an adult as a white kid under the identical circumstances.[18]

In the early 1990s Gary Graham adopted the nom de guerre of Shaka Sankofa, and the rage that got him thrown in jail in the first place was refocused on the Texas criminal justice system. Proclaiming his innocence to any and all comers, he has slowly gathered supporters and they now range from local activists to Italian parliamentarians. Jesse Jackson is demanding a stay of the execution. So is the U.N. High Commissioner for Human Rights.[19] The *New York Times* and the *Manchester Guardian* have reporters en route to death row in Huntsville, Texas.

There, the press corps finds a gaunt and intense 36-year-old facing them through the bulletproof window of the visitor's cubicle. His voice rasps through the telephone in the staccato rhythm of a man in a hurry. "I'm hoping," he says, "with the support of the people, I'll have many more years to do positive things." He says he is determined to get off death row "by any means necessary."

Dick Burr's partner, Mandy Welch, is among the visitors. She has been coming here for a dozen years, but she and Graham are still not close. "He doesn't go around expressing a lot of appreciation and making sure that he's nice to people," she says. "But if he'd have been that kind of person I'm not sure that he could have survived.... He sort of has a revolutionary personality. He thinks that he has the capacity of helping people and changing things. The cause has become more important than anything else. And I think there's a lot to admire in that."

HOUSTON—MAY 4, 2000

The fax machine in Dick Burr's office is so often the bearer of bad news that he and Mandy are always braced for the worst. But as they scan the order from the Supreme Court there is a sinking sense of finality: "The petition for writ of certiorari is denied." In refusing to review the New Orleans decision, the High Court essentially affirms that the federal judiciary is prohibited by the Anti-terrorism and Effective Death Penalty Act of 1996 from considering the additional eyewitnesses because Ron Mock could have introduced them at the time of the trial and he didn't.

"They really are sort of looking at the number of angels on the head of a pin," says Burr. "They've lost sight as a body of what's important here."

Once again there's no time for hand-wringing. The new execution date is June 22.

AUSTIN—
THURSDAY, JUNE 15, 2000—D-MINUS-7

Colonel Jack Zimmerman was a Marine Corps vet with a couple of Bronze Stars for valor before he got into private law practice. He brings battle-honed discipline and tenacity to the job, and his courtroom record has pushed Zimmerman & Lavine to the top rank of criminal law firms in Houston. When Dick Burr asked Zimmerman for advice on the Gary Graham case a few years back, Jack agreed to come on board as an unpaid consultant because he thought the state's refusal to hear these witnesses was outrageous. Since the first of the year his involvement has deepened day by day and now

Zimmerman's firm is working nearly full time with Burr & Welch in a desperate last-ditch effort to save Graham.

The lethal needle is now just seven days away. Only two possibilities remain: Governor Bush and/or the Texas Board of Pardons and Paroles. Burr and Zimmerman catch a plane for the capitol in Austin. They've arranged a meeting with the governor's counsel, Margaret Wilson, and tomorrow they'll be seeing the chairman of the Board of Pardon's and Paroles. On the flight up they go over the pitch one more time even though they could now do it in their sleep.

The general counsel's office is in the State Insurance building which has been largely taken over by the governor. Margaret Wilson is joined there by a couple of aides and a former Houston assistant D.A. who now works for Governor Bush. Both the D.A. and Ms. Wilson are well up on the case. They know the record and their questions are penetrating.

They are skeptical about the new eyewitnesses. They point out that Sherian Etuk's recent statements do not jibe with what she originally told the cops. The police report says that she heard the gunshot and saw somebody fleeing, but that she didn't see his face.

Burr says the record is clearly mistaken. After the shooting, the police took Ms. Etuk to the station and showed her a photo array and asked her to identify the killer. Why would they do that unless she had seen his face? Clearly the police left something out of the report, says Burr, and what they left out was the half hour before the shooting when Sherian Etuk saw the killer up close.

The governor's people are unmoved. In addition to doubts about the eyewitnesses, they have problems with Graham's revolutionary statements. A year ago, he wrote a manifesto about his views of the world and at one point he talked about people rallying to stop his execution "by any means necessary." If his execution is delayed, they fear, he will just have more time to foment violence.

Dismayed by their open admission that Graham's personal politics are a factor in deciding whether to let the man have a hearing or kill him first, Burr bites his tongue and tries to calm their fears. He says the statement was written last year when Gary was facing an imminent execution date. "That's been the way he's coped with being there," says Burr. "He's become a revolutionary. I think he's a deluded revolutionary —"

"Sort of like you," says Wilson.

Burr looks at her. "No," he says. "You're the one who's deluded."

"Oh, I meant, you're a revolutionary."

"I'm a peacemaker," says Burr.

Peacemaker or not, after three hours on this griddle he is disheartened. The palpable disgust these people feel toward Graham seems bomb-proof. But on the way out of the building, Jack Zimmerman tries to be upbeat. True, he says, the questioning was hostile, but it's Margaret Wilson's job to play devil's advocate. At least she knew the details so the decision won't be made out of ignorance.[20]

HOUSTON—THURSDAY—D-MINUS-7

One of the innocent victims of the Gary Graham debacle is the original heroine, Bernadine Skillern. Since that day in court nineteen years ago when she identified Gary Graham as the killer, her life has been turned upside down. First she got death threats from people in her own community and had to quit her job because of the controversy and the harassment. Then she tried to drop out of sight and get on with her life. But every time Gary Graham's number comes up, the press has tracked her down. Tomorrow morning her picture will be spread across three columns in the *New York Times*.[21]

Seated in her lawyer's office at a long table facing the television cameras, Bernadine Skillern wipes a tear from her eye as she recounts that horrible night yet again. She agreed to this press conference because she wants the public to hear her side of the argument. The news has been dominated lately by death penalty critics and Gary Graham supporters. Bernadine Skillern feels it's time to set the record straight. Who better to do that than the woman who saw Gary Graham pull the trigger?

This kind of pressure might overwhelm a lesser person, but Bernadine Skillern is no ordinary person. Solid as a rock, she says Gary Graham is the man she saw that night. There is not the slightest doubt about that. "I saw Mr. Graham shoot and kill Mr. Lambert in that parking lot in 1981," she says. "That has not changed. That is not going to change."[22]

For the average viewer watching this courageous woman on the six o'clock news, that's enough to settle the issue. Bernadine Skillern's unshakable certainty is so powerful it seems to sweep all arguments aside just as it did at the trial 18 years ago. This woman looked directly at the killer's face twice—once only a few yards away.

But two days later in the Sunday edition of the *New York Times* there is a chilling reminder that Bernadine Skillern's absolute certainty could be resting on quicksand. In an op-ed piece titled, "I Was Certain but I Was Wrong," a North Carolina woman tells a horrifying tale of mistaken identity.

Sixteen years ago, writes Jennifer Thompson, she was

raped in her college dorm. Resistance was out of the question—he had a knife at her throat—so she decided to concentrate on making sure the sonofabitch never did this again.[23]

"I studied every single detail on the rapist's face," she says. "I looked at his hairline; I looked for scars, for tattoos, for anything that would help me identify him. When and if I survived the attack, I was going to make sure that he was put in prison and he was going to rot."

She did survive, and with the help of the police she dug through a mountain of mug shots until she finally spotted him. Beyond a shadow of doubt, this was the face. His name was Ronald Cotton.

She also picked Cotton out of a lineup a few days later, and her testimony in court sent him to prison for life. "It was the happiest day of my life," says Thompson, "I could begin to put it all behind me."

But it never seems to work that way. The case was overturned on appeal and she had to go through the whole nightmare again. And during this trial, the defense introduced some new evidence. It seems some other guy—a man in prison with her attacker—was bragging that he had committed the rape. So they brought this man into the courtroom and presented him to Jennifer.

"Ms. Thompson, have you ever seen this man?"

"I have never seen him in my life," she said. "I have no idea who he is."

Once again Ronald Cotton was sentenced to life, this time for good. "He was never going to get out," she says. "He was never going to hurt another woman."

Jennifer Thompson somehow recovered and managed to get on with her life. She got married, started a family, and began doing volunteer work with abused children.

But Cotton's lawyers were indefatigable. Eight years later they were back again, this time asking Jennifer for a sample of her DNA. Hairs and other evidence from the crime scene were going to be tested to see who matched what. She complied immediately, thankful at last that science could put an end to this madness once and for all.

A few weeks later she was standing in her kitchen—she remembers it vividly—and one of the detectives stopped by to see her. He had the district attorney with him. They told her she had made a mistake. It was the other guy who raped her, not Ronald Cotton.

"The man I was so sure I had never seen in my life was the man who was inches from my throat," she says. "And the man I had identified so emphatically on so many occasions was absolutely innocent."

Thunderstruck by the realization that her word had shackled the wrong man for eleven years, Jennifer Thompson is now on a crusade. "If anything good can come out of what Ronald Cotton suffered because of my limitations as a human being, let it be an awareness of the fact that eyewitnesses can and do make mistakes." Her warning underscores the fundamental weakness in the case against Gary Graham. He was convicted on the testimony of a single eyewitness. There was no physical evidence.

Today, Jennifer Thompson and Ronald Cotton have somehow managed to bridge the unbridgeable. They've even become friends. But she lives with the knowledge that for eleven years, while she was getting married and raising a family, he was in a cell. She has a word of warning for Governor Bush.

"Today there is a man in Texas named Gary Graham who is about to be executed," she writes, "because one witness is confident that Mr. Graham is the killer she saw from

30 to 40 feet away. This woman saw the murderer for only a fraction of the time that I saw the man who raped me." She acknowledges that Bernadine Skillern's certainty is unshakable. "But she cannot possibly be any more positive than I was about Ronald Cotton. What if she is dead wrong?"

HOUSTON—
TUESDAY, JUNE 20—1:00 P.M.—D-MINUS-2

Bianca Jagger is in town representing Amnesty International. She and Jesse Jackson are addressing a crowd of several hundred supporters at an anti-death penalty rally in Houston's Fifth Ward.

On the other side of town in a tinted-glass office complex on South Post Oak Lane, Jack Zimmerman's conference room is filling with camera crews and reporters. The execution is two days away. With no hint yet from the governor or the Board, Dick Burr and Jack Zimmerman are taking the case to the people. This hastily-called press conference was pulled together this morning to take advantage of a slip-up by the state's top lawman last night on Nightline.

During an interview with ABC's Chris Bury, Texas Attorney General John Cornyn seemed to display a fundamental misunderstanding of the Graham case. Bury asked Cornyn why these new eyewitnesses, Sherian Etuk and Ronald Hubbard, had never had a chance to tell their story to a judge. "They've never been questioned in open court," said Bury, "they've never been cross-examined, they've never had a jury hear what it is they have to say."

Cornyn disagreed. He said they had been heard. "Indeed, after Mr. Graham's lawyers identified these supposed eyewitnesses—some 12 years after the trial in this case—they were heard by a judge in open court and found to lack credibility."

This is patently false. Etuk and Hubbard have never been heard by a judge anywhere, says Zimmerman. "The Attorney General is absolutely one-hundred percent wrong. If his opposition to clemency is based on his mistaken belief that these witnesses have been heard, then clemency is clearly in order."

Attorney General Cornyn and his people say that these witnesses wouldn't have made any difference anyway because Bernadine Skillern's identification was so powerful. But Zimmerman has some news for Cornyn about the credibility of these new eyewitnesses. He and Burr videotaped the statements of Etuk and Hubbard, then they tracked down three of the original jurors. After watching the tapes, all three jurors signed affidavits saying that these witnesses would have changed the outcome of the trial.

Zimmerman hands out copies of the affidavits and the reporters snap them up.

"...I do not understand why Gary Graham's lawyer did not bring those witnesses in to testify...If Etuk and Hubbard had testified at the trial...I would have had a serious doubt about him being guilty..."

"...If I had known that Mr. Graham was the only man in the live lineup whose photograph had also been shown to Bernadine Skillern the day before, it would have helped explain why she might have been mistaken...I would not have been able to convict Gary Graham on the evidence..."

"...There was no smoking gun. There were no fingerprints. No physical evidence was presented that tied Gary Graham to the crime...I have viewed the videotape...What they had to say causes me to have a doubt about Bernadine Skillern's testimony..."[24]

If any one of these jurors had expressed these doubts back in 1981, says Zimmerman, Gary Graham would not be on death row tonight.

But during the Q&A, it becomes clear that the convoluted history of the Graham case is beyond the reach of the average reporter on a deadline. A TV newsman from one of the major local stations seems resolutely confused. Referring to the Attorney General's statement on Nightline, he says, "I think their argument is, it's already been tried in court and been through the appeals process—"

Zimmerman pounds the table. "It hasn't been tried in court! Nobody has heard these witnesses."

"But Judge Shipley did hear two of them, did he not?

Now Burr leaps up. "He did not hear eyewitnesses!"

"He didn't hear two witnesses?"

"He heard two alibi witnesses," says Burr. "Please! Get the difference. An alibi witness says 'the person was with me somewhere else.' An eyewitness says, 'I saw somebody commit a crime and this is what they look like.' No eyewitness that would have helped Gary Graham has ever been heard in court. None."

"Okay, well, that statement means that alibi witnesses wouldn't help Gary Graham, I mean—"

"No!" says Burr. "I said no eyewitnesses. Please, do not misinterpret what I'm saying. Three alibi witnesses testified in February 1988 and Judge Shipley found they were not credible. We are not putting forward alibi witnesses. There's a difference between an alibi witness and an eyewitness like night and day! Please, get it straight!"

That's easier said than done. Another reporter picks up the same thread. "Mr. Burr, what would you say to those folks that, I guess you'd say are on the other side of this case, who would say what you and the other attorneys have not been able to do in court, you're now trying to do through public relations?"

Burr looks at him wearily. "We have no place else to go. The court system has utterly failed Gary Graham. It is a miserable testament to the integrity of the judicial system in this country that no judge has heard these witnesses. It is a shame! The people who should be blamed are the courts. They have dropped the ball, they have refused to do what justice required. They are to blame. We have no where else to go."

HUNTSVILLE—TUESDAY—4:00 P.M.—D-MINUS-2

Jack Zimmerman has to stay in Houston to attend a press conference with Jesse Jackson so Dick Burr heads up to death row alone.

Huntsville, Texas, is in the rolling green hills an hour north of Houston. The climate here is much more tolerable, which is why Sam Houston chose to live in Huntsville rather than the coastal swamp that was named for him. Sam Houston built a house in town that looks exactly like a river steamboat—he loved yanking everybody's chain—but the great Texan's notorious eccentricity seems jarringly out of place alongside Huntsville's other main attraction. A few blocks east along these tree-shaded streets the view is interrupted by an awesome red brick fortress known as "The Walls." Built in the 1800s as the state's first prison, it was intended to look forbidding and it succeeds. Thirty-foot ramparts interrupted by watchtowers enclose an area of six city blocks on a hill right in the middle of town. Because of its age, it's no longer suitable for the inmates of death row, but it still houses the state's execution chamber in a low

building beneath the northwest watchtower. Unless Dick
Burr can somehow stop the steamroller, this sterile cubicle
will be Gary Graham's final destination in about 48 hours.

Condemned prisoners used to be stored at The Walls
back in the days of "Old Sparky," the state's electric chair, but
now they're located in a maximum security prison 40 miles
east in Livingston. It's there that Dick Burr joins the stream
of newsmen, religious leaders and political activists trooping
in to see Graham as the clock runs down. The lawyer finds
his client vibrating with energy and anger.

Graham, like a man with terminal cancer, has been at
death's door so often he's lost count, but each time Dick Burr
and his team have somehow managed to stop the clock. It's
almost impossible to believe they can't do it again. Graham
is clinging to that hope. But at the same time he's preparing
to go out like a revolutionary. He will resist, he says. They
will not lead him down that hall like a goat. He will fight
them every inch of the way.

Burr believes there's room for hope. He says that the
Board of Pardons and Paroles is now saying they won't
announce their decision on clemency until noon on
Thursday—six hours before the execution—but that could
be a good sign since they're taking so long to make up their
minds. On the other hand, Burr's job is to anticipate the
worst. He says he's going to lodge a new petition with the
U.S. Supreme Court tomorrow. That way the Justices will
already have the papers in their hands in case he has to call
on them for a last minute intervention.

Finally, Burr asks Graham if he wants him to be here on
Thursday in the event that everything goes wrong. Graham
laughs. "No, I want you to be in Houston working. If they
execute me, you don't deserve to be here."

Driving back to Houston, Burr feels like he's been in the ring for sixteen rounds. He is apprehensive about the Board of Pardons and Paroles and he doesn't feel all that much better about the Supreme Court. Governor Bush has been tight lipped—another bad sign. The last time Bush granted a reprieve there was a lot of advance warning out of Austin.

The truth is, Governor Bush has very little maneuvering room in this situation even if he wanted to intervene, which he clearly does not. If he knuckled under to a bunch of bleeding hearts like Bianca Jagger and Jesse Jackson, his core constituency would be on fire. And since everybody seems to understand that, the only thing left for reporters to discuss is the Governor's demeanor.

The press is defining the issue as "gravitas." Does George Bush have the intellectual weight to handle the job? The question cropped up last year when *Talk* magazine published a controversial profile that had Bush mocking the last-minute clemency plea of Karla Faye Tucker. It flared up again during the primary debates. Bush was told about a Texas lawyer who slept through a trial that led to a death sentence and he laughed. It may have been nervous laughter but it was the wrong response.[25]

Tomorrow morning's New York Times will weigh in on the subject with a quote from Georgetown University professor Stephen Wayne: "This gravitas issue is a very important one. I don't think he can say, in a snide way, 'I'm going through with this, he's guilty, period.' He's got to demonstrate some reflection in his words."[26]

Above all, he must not come across as vulnerable to public pressure like his Democratic opponent Al Gore. "The most important thing for him to do is remain consistent," says Republican strategist Don Sipple.

So the Governor's role is fairly circumscribed. He must exhibit gravitas, but beyond that he'd be insane to get involved with this tar-baby. What's more, he doesn't have to. He can't grant clemency on his own. Only the Board of Pardons and Paroles can do that. And while the governor can grant a 30-day reprieve, he can grant only one reprieve per customer. Since Governor Ann Richards already granted a stay back in 1993, Bush takes the position that Graham's ticket has already been punched.

HOUSTON—
WEDNESDAY, JUNE 21—3:00 A.M.—D-MINUS-1

In the dead of night Dick Burr's face is illuminated by the glow of the computer screen. The phone has finally stopped jumping off the hook and Burr is taking advantage of the silence for one more pass at his final Hail-Mary petition to the Supreme Court. His argument is simple: if the Court, in an extraordinary case, has the constitutional authority to ignore the Effective Death Penalty Act, then this is such a case. But if the law says the Court no longer has this authority, then isn't the law itself unconstitutional in granting excess power to the Legislative branch?

Sounds logical, but lately the high court has been following a logic of its own on the death penalty. Either way, it will be a close call. Burr can count on four votes: John Paul Stevens, Ruth Bader Ginsberg, Stephen Bryer, and David Souter. On the other side of the moat will be Chief Justice Rehnquist with Anthony Kennedy, Clarence Thomas, and Antonin Scalia. This leaves the ball in the hands of Justice Sandra Day O'Connor. Her normal inclination is to vote with Scalia and the Chief Justice but you never know. She could go either way.

By the time Burr prints out the final draft, daylight is filtering through the towering shade trees along Castle Court, and as Burr's young intern races for Houston International with the documents in the seat beside him, the temperature and humidity are on their way back up to the century mark. The flight attendant on the American flight to Washington will act as courier. Within hours, copies of the petition will be in the hands of each of the nine justices, on hold until they get word from Graham's attorneys. When push comes to shove, Burr will be able to activate the new petition for a stay of execution with a single phone call.

AUSTIN—WEDNESDAY—D-MINUS-1

The Texas Board of Pardons and Paroles now holds Gary Graham's life in its hands and for anyone who's at all concerned about his continued good health, that's not a happy prospect. In the last five years, the Board has heard 68 appeals for clemency. They've given a thumbs-up only once.

This inscrutable organization consists of eighteen Texans appointed by the governor and they work full time for the state at a salary of $80,000 a year. Not surprisingly a lot of them are active Republicans and most have backgrounds in law enforcement. But there is also a rancher, an ex-schoolteacher and a psychologist. They spend the majority of their time deciding whether or not to grant parole to robbers, car thieves and drug users, but it's also their job to deal with clemency appeals from death row.

Curiously, the board members almost never assemble in the same room. Because the state is so vast, they divvy up the cases and handle them semi-autonomously from various regional offices. In death penalty cases, however, the whole board must be involved because a majority—ten votes—is required for clemency. Yet even then they do not physically meet. Some members discuss it on the phone, some don't, but they deliberate individually, then fax their votes to the chairman's office in Austin.

With the national spotlight now focused on the state's legal machinery, there is growing criticism of the board and its enigmatic operations. Two years ago legislation was introduced in Austin that would have forced the board to hold clemency hearings in public but Governor Bush vetoed it. He was afraid it might create "a chance for people to rant and rail, a chance for people to emotionalize the process beyond the questions that need to be asked."[27]

From a defense attorney's point of view, the board's procedures are maddening. Ideally, you would like to get all eighteen members in a room somewhere and make your pitch and have them vote. But since they don't actually get together, Burr and Zimmerman had to make their case privately to Board Chairman Gerald Garrett in Austin last Friday. Garrett then agreed to forward copies of their brief to the other board members. Included in the package are videotaped affidavits from Sherian Etuk and Ron Hubbard along with affidavits from the three jurors who say the testimony would have changed their vote. But in this strange virtual courtroom, there's no way to know if any of the judges will actually look at this evidence.

HOUSTON—WEDNESDAY—D-MINUS-1

Surprisingly, the quest for Bobby Lambert's killer turned out to be fertile turf. Burr's investigators pursued the hit-man angle and found that Lambert was indeed being squeezed by the feds. "We learned that the FBI wanted Lambert to testify against a fellow in northwest Oklahoma," says Burr. It seems that when Lambert and his copilot were busted with a plane-load of illegal drugs, the police neglected to get a search warrant so the evidence was suppressed. With the case against Lambert and his partner suddenly crippled, the feds started focusing on a third guy who was said to be the money behind the operation. "They started pushing them [Lambert and his partner] to turn on the third guy," says Burr. "And Lambert said he didn't want to do it because he was afraid of the guy."

When Lambert turned up dead a short time later, the federal agents in Oklahoma didn't pursue the hit-man angle because they were told that Lambert had been killed by Gary Graham in a botched stick-up.

For a defendant to claim that somebody else murdered the victim over a drug deal is hardly an original dodge. But when Burr's investigators contact the lawyer who was representing Bobby Lambert at the time, he says he has no doubt his client was bumped off to keep him from testifying.[28]

The investigators have uncovered several other tantalizing leads but they've run out of time. None of this will make any difference unless the clock can be stopped.

DEATH ROW—
WEDNESDAY—5:00 P.M.—D-MINUS-1

Gary Graham has just finished an interview and he's on the way back to his cell when he's suddenly surrounded by prison guards in battle gear. Graham has consistently maintained that he will not go to the slab willingly, so the Department of Corrections has opted for a preemptive strike. Taken by surprise in the narrow corridor, Graham struggles but it's no contest. He's quickly subdued, chained hand and foot, and hustled out of the building.

The transfer from Livingston to The Walls in

Huntsville had been scheduled for noon tomorrow but Warden Glen Castlebury and his men wanted to avoid the difficulty and danger of forcibly removing Graham from his cell. They're obviously going to have to grapple with him tomorrow to get him into the death chamber at The Walls but there's no sense doing it twice.

There's also the issue of security. Graham's growing army of supporters now includes radical left-wing groups like the New Black Panthers. With threats hanging in the air about stopping the execution "by any means necessary" and with a sizeable army of protesters expected in the streets around the prison tomorrow, Castlebury's not taking any chances.

A squad of troopers and guards hustle Graham into a van and head out in an armed convoy with a chopper over-head. In less than an hour he's safely inside the death house in Huntsville and locked down in a holding cell next door to the execution chamber. After things settle down, they offer him dinner. He refuses. According to Rev. Jackson, "He does not want to eat on the table of those who would kill him."[29]

HOUSTON—
THURSDAY, JUNE 22—8:00 A.M.—D-DAY

With the execution set for 6:00 p.m., Jack Zimmerman's office on South Post Oak Lane has become the eleventh-hour command post for the Graham defense team. Dick Burr and Mandy Welch just got here. Dick just came from a 6:00 a.m. slot on Good Morning America followed by a run to the airport to ship one final appeal to the state's top court in Austin. Burr holds no real hope for that effort—the odds are zero that the Texas Court of Criminal Appeals will have a last minute change of heart about Gary Graham—but Burr promised his client he would pursue every avenue.

Zimmerman's office is already filling with supporters

and legal experts from around the country. Outside the press is unpacking their gear and among the network television crews is a sprinkling of young European documentarians with their mini-digital cameras and anguished faces. "What's going on in this country?" asks a stunned Finnish camerawoman. "There is something wrong with the system!"

Everybody in the office is listening to the radio or monitoring the fax machine, waiting for the word from the Board of Pardons and Paroles. The phones are ringing off the hook and not all the calls are friendly. The other side is weighing in. One caller says, "Dick Burr, you're a lying sonofabitch," but so far no death threats.

Yesterday the state filed a response to Burr's latest Supreme Court petition and Burr is faxing a response to their response when he gets another call. It's the *New York Times*. The reporter says that the Board of Pardons and Paroles has denied clemency. "We heard you lost twelve to five. Do you have anything to say?"

Burr says he hasn't heard anything but he's willing to admit that the leak is probably accurate. Twenty minutes later a fax from Austin confirms it.

Zimmerman calls the governor's counsel, Margaret Wilson, on the off chance that her boss might grant a last-minute reprieve, but she confirms that he's more likely to walk on the moon. So the next two calls are to the Supreme Court in Washington and the Court of Criminal Appeals in Austin asking them to act on the petitions they already have in hand.

Then Burr calls his client to let him know what's going on. Graham, tense but still in control, refuses to give up. He still believes somehow he'll get through this. Burr says they will keep fighting. This is the last call Burr will be able to

make unless he is successful. With a final word of encourage-
ment, he says goodbye.

Then he and Zimmerman go outside to face the press.[30]

HUNTSVILLE—THURSDAY—11:30 A.M.—D-DAY

Flak-jacketed police in riot gear are patrolling the
perimeter of The Walls with the Texas Rangers and National
Guard standing in reserve. The street in front of the prison
has been cordoned off to separate the pro- and anti-Graham
demonstrators, and the press has been corralled between the
two camps on a tree-shaded lawn directly opposite the main
entrance.

Along the sidewalk facing the old fortress, a collection
of tent-like canvas flys have been staked out to protect the
TV reporters from the blistering sun. With the temperature
already into the 90s and the humidity moving up with it, the
makeup artists are having a hard time keeping their on-cam-
era stars from melting. A production assistant places a cold
towel on the back of Geraldo's neck as he rattles an update
into a cell phone.

The crowd of thousands that the authorities had feared
turns out to be a crowd of about five hundred but that's small
consolation to Warden Castlebury since it includes both the
Ku Klux Klan and the New Black Panthers. The Panthers—
armed black militants—are a particular concern because in
Texas it's perfectly legal to walk down Main Street carrying a
weapon as long as it's not concealed, and the Panthers have
no interest in concealing their weapons. So the state police
have invoked a two-block no-gun buffer zone around the
prison, and so far the overwhelming presence of lawmen with
riot shields is enough to keep the outraged protesters confined to speeches and flag burning. Through the afternoon

the rasp of bull horns and tom-toms and chants of "Free Sankofa!" echo off the 30-foot red brick walls that surround him.

When the KKK finally makes its entrance, it's a disappointment to the camera crews. The Klan's once fearsome presence has been reduced to a couple of white boys with hoods and Confederate flags followed by a handful of boosters. They join a dozen blue collar workers sweating it out in the pro-death penalty camp. And here is a group of clean-cut white kids from Sam Houston State College who feel Gary Graham should have been executed a long time ago.

"He was found guilty in thirty-three appellate courts," says Amanda.

The others agree. "I think they should kill him," says Brian.

But one of the girls isn't so sure. "I have mixed emotions. If he is innocent, I mean, that's bad. I mean, I feel sorry for him. However, he did attempt to shoot three other people."

That's the factor that seems to doom Graham in the eyes of most Texans, judiciary included. If he is innocent of this particular crime, he's guilty of a bunch of others. Says Emily, a young sorority girl in a Chi Omega T-shirt, "To me it doesn't make any difference. But I think he's guilty."

HOUSTON—THURSDAY—4:30 P.M.—D-DAY

Zimmerman and Burr are on hold. There's nothing left to do but wait for the word from Washington and pray that Sandra Day O'Connor sees the light. One encouraging sign: the court is taking a long time—so long that the state has just set the execution back an hour to 7:00 p.m.

A few minutes before 5:00 there's a call for Burr and the

ball is suddenly back in the air. It's an attorney from Austin who occasionally lends a hand on the case. He tells Burr that he was at the health club near the Capitol and he ran into Judge James Nowlin of the federal district court. The judge told him he's been following the case and he thinks that Gary Graham may have a legitimate beef. Nowlin said that if Graham's lawyers can come up with a plausible reason to delay the execution on civil rights grounds, he'll grant a stay. The judge said he was going back to his chambers and he'd wait there until he heard from Burr one way or the other.

Suddenly everybody's in motion. As Zimmerman and Burr huddle with the experts already on board, staffers are reaching out to constitutional authorities around the country. They've got about ninety minutes to come up with a brand new reason why the federal government should halt this execution on civil rights grounds, and that's no easy task. This field has been well-plowed. The Supreme Court has already slapped down several recent attempts to use this strategy, but with an invitation like this, you can't turn it down.

After an hour of frantic labor they get the word from Washington they've been dreading. The Supreme Court has split as predicted, and Justice Sandra Day O'Connor voted with the Rehnquist faction, tilting the balance against Graham five to four. They did not deny his petition for a hearing, they just denied him a stay of execution.

This blow is quickly followed by the denial from the Court of Criminal Appeals in Austin. Suddenly the offer from Judge Nowlin looms much larger. It's all that's left. The execution is now less than an hour away.

In an attempt to stop the clock, they print out what they have in hand and fax it to Austin. It's a patchwork quilt stitched together from pieces of other appeals and at one point Burr realizes they've got some other prisoner's name in the thing. It's got to be one of the sloppiest presentations ever filed but it does the trick. The state once more must bring the steamroller to a halt. As long as there is a court proceeding pending anywhere the execution cannot go forward.

The argument Burr and Zimmerman are advancing in these final hours is not some arcane constitutional sleight of hand, but instead has to do with simple fairness. They're alleging that the State of Texas violated Gary Graham's civil rights because the secretive clemency process is based on luck and whimsey rather than due process. To prove the point, Burr describes a phone call he got just last night. Charles Shipman, a member of the Board of Pardons and Paroles, called from Lubbock looking for information. He had been digging through the case files and had become intrigued with Graham's alibi witnesses. Shipman wanted to know the details of a rock concert that took place in Houston the weekend after the murder. It seems one of the alibi witnesses had placed the night they were with Gary Graham in relation to that concert. Shipman said, "I called a Houston Chronicle reporter trying to get this information," but he was unsuccessful.

Burr said, "It sounds like you all need some people helping you."

"Oh, yeah, you know, we have to do all this ourselves."

Burr looked up the information and Shipman apparently decided that the alibi was credible—he was one of the five board members who would later vote to commute Graham's sentence. But the reason Burr is passing along this anecdote is to get Judge Nowlin to focus on the Keystone Cops nature of this process. Here was a member of the Board of Pardons and Paroles calling the Houston Chronicle looking for facts that might save a man's life. Clearly this rinky-dink phone and fax arrangement needs to be opened up to public view and the board must be forced to assemble in one place and hammer out a decision after everybody has the same information.

Unfortunately, this argument won't fly. Judge Nowlin says the Supreme Court has already rejected this line of reasoning because there's no inherent constitutional right to clemency. It's up to the states to grant it or not. Whatever the process, how they go about it is their business.

But the judge still isn't ready to give up. He asks them to try again. If they can come up with anything else, he'll be standing by.

HUNTSVILLE—THURSDAY—5:30 P.M.—D-DAY

The State of Texas knows full well what's going on here. If Graham's lawyers can keep this ball in the air until midnight, the designated execution date will have passed and their client will get an automatic 30-day reprieve. From the state's viewpoint, this would be bad news indeed. This is Gary Graham's eighth date with the needle. Tempers on the street are already boiling and every day this mess drags on makes it more likely that somebody will get hurt. But until they get the go ahead, all they can do is keep the machinery on hair-trigger alert.

Graham has refused all food and drink for the last day-and-a-half and he's made it clear he will fight them to the end. Since he refuses to cooperate, Castlebury threatens to limit his visitors, but you can hardly leave Bianca Jagger and Jesse Jackson cooling their heels in the lobby. They've been in to see Graham and so has his spiritual advisor, Minister Robert Muhammad of the Nation of Islam in Houston. Graham's even-tempered intensity masks a well of anger but the final reality is beginning to sink in. If the execution goes forward, Graham says, he wants Jesse and Bianca to be there.

HOUSTON—THURSDAY—7:00 P.M.—D-DAY

For the next half hour Burr and Zimmerman struggle to come up with some way through the maze but every corridor is blocked. For another twenty minutes they argue about the possibility of getting a stay from the Fifth Circuit in New Orleans, but without a new angle they won't be able to keep the dance going long enough to get past midnight. The judges in the Fifth Circuit have been alerted and they're undoubtedly standing by the phones. Unless Burr and his team can come up with an absolutely brand new argument, the federal appellate court will slam the ball back in their faces within minutes.

Burr notifies Judge Nowlin that they have hit the wall. Nowlin reluctantly dismisses the suit. A few minutes later the attorney general's office calls to see if Burr has any other tricks up his sleeve.

Like an Indy driver running out of gas in the final lap, Burr realizes it's over. For seven years he has struggled to out-run the executioner. Over the last month-and-a-half he's been at it fifteen hours a day without letup. He is pulverized. And he has failed.

The attorney general needs an answer. Burr says, "We plan no further appeals."

AUSTIN—THURSDAY—8:00 P.M.—D-DAY

It's been a long day for Governor Bush. Called back from the campaign trail, he's been in his office since early this morning dealing with a backlog of state business and standing by for this moment. He steps up to the microphone with a prepared statement.

"Over the last 19 years, Mr. Graham's case has been reviewed more than 20 times by state and federal courts. Thirty-three judges have heard and found his numerous claims to be without merit.

"In addition to the extensive due process provided Mr. Graham through the courts, the Board of Pardons and Paroles has thoroughly reviewed the record of this case as well as all new claims raised by Mr. Graham's lawyers. Today the Board of Pardons and Paroles voted to allow Mr. Graham's execution to go forward. I support the board's decision.

"Mr. Graham has had full and fair access to state and federal courts, including the United States Supreme Court.

"After considering all the facts, I am confident justice is being done. May God bless the victims, the families of the victims, and may God bless Mr. Graham."

HOUSTON—THURSDAY 22—8:00 P.M.—D-DAY

Dick Burr is dead on his feet as he faces the cameras one more time. Defeated, he looks haggard and aged. But he's unbowed. "Because of human error, human frailty, and no will to acknowledge our own frailty, we are about to put to death a man who is innocent. There is no greater miscarriage of justice, or travesty, or horror that a state can do to one of its citizens than this."[31]

HUNTSVILLE—THURSDAY—8:00 P.M.—D-DAY

True to his word, Shaka Sankofa goes down swinging. Cornered in his cell, he struggles with all his might but the armor-plated extraction team has had plenty of practice and they quickly overwhelm him.

Outside, the press corps has been largely in the dark about the end game. But when they spot Jesse Jackson and Bianca Jagger among the cluster of dignitaries heading for the main entrance, they realize something's up.

The witnesses for the condemned man and the victim are ushered in separately so they don't bump into each other in the hall. Each group has its own tiny cubicle overlooking the death chamber. On the victim's side there is Bobby Lambert's grandson and one of the robbery victims that Graham wounded in a separate incident back in 1981. Attorney Roe Wilson is here representing the Harris County district attorney's office, and with her is the woman who has been pushing for this execution harder than anyone, Dianne Clements of Justice for All.

In the other cubicle Rev. Jackson and Bianca Jagger are joined by Minister Robert Muhammad and Rev. Al Sharpton, a few prison officials, and the pool reporters from AP, UPI and the *Huntsville Item* who witness every execution.[32]

The curtains are pulled back and there is Shaka Sankofa on the gurney, arms outstretched as if on a cross. It's obvious that he kept his promise to "fight like hell." In addition to all the regular straps and belts, they've had to jury-rig a restraint for his head. Last night he refused to be strip-searched, so he was not allowed to wear regular clothes. The paper suit they gave him ripped in the struggle so they've covered him with a sheet. The needle is already in his vein.

A microphone hangs from the ceiling to capture his last words. He is nervous but his voice is clear as he speaks in rapid-fire staccato.

"I would like to say that I did not kill Bobby Lambert. That I'm an innocent black man that is being murdered. This is a lynching that is happening in America tonight. There's overwhelming and compelling evidence of my defense that has never been heard in any court of America. What is happening here is an outrage for any civilized country."

For six minutes he ranges through a mix of revolutionary rhetoric and personal thoughts, literally putting off the terrible moment one sentence at a time. He thanks all the people who have rallied to his cause and he urges them to keep up the struggle. "We must not let this murder-lynching be forgotten tonight, my brothers. We must take it to the nation. We must keep our faith. We must go forward."

He has unkind words for the State of Texas. "They know I'm innocent. They've got the facts to prove it. They know I'm innocent. But they cannot acknowledge my innocence, because to do so would be to publicly admit their guilt."

The pool reporters for AP and UPI are struggling to take down every word because there are several hundred people on deadline outside who are depending on them for quotes. Finally Graham says, "Keep marching Black People. They are killing me tonight. They are murdering me tonight."

With that the I.V. valves are opened and a cocktail of sedatives, muscle relaxants and heart stopping potassium chloride begins filtering into his bloodstream.

Outside, the lighted clock face above the prison entrance reads 8:49.

NEW YORK—THE FOLLOWING DAY—
FRIDAY, JUNE 23, 2000

On the issue of gravitas, the *New York Times* gives Governor Bush a pass: "Mr. Bush spoke in a somber voice and wore a solemn expression as he delivered a written statement about the case. He did not make eye contact with reporters, as he typically does, and walked briskly in and out of the room. He did not take questions."

HOUSTON—FRIDAY, JUNE 23—2000

Attorney Stephen Bright, director of the Southern Center for Human Rights in Atlanta, happens to be in Houston today for a long-scheduled address to the Harris County Criminal Lawyers Association. Bright says that Gary Graham may someday accomplish in death what eluded him in life. "When the history is written of the eventual abandonment of the death penalty in the United States...the name and case of Gary Graham will figure very prominently because the American people have been watching this case. They have come to the realization that the criminal justice system does not work...and that it makes deadly errors."

Bright's certainty about the ultimate fate of the death penalty seems to be supported by the historic trend toward moderation in punishment. It's been a long time since we hung anyone in chains from a gibbet. Where once there was only one rule—the king's word—today there is a thicket of rules to protect the accused. But as we are about to see, the authority of the court then, as now, has always taken precedence over simple justice. Process becomes paramount, and if the process has been followed correctly, innocence may still be irrelevant.

> *"There is no basis... for finding in the Constitution a right to demand judicial consideration of newly discovered evidence of innocence brought forward after conviction."*
> —U.S. Supreme Court Justice Antonin Scalia[33]

CHAPTER TWO

*"Excessive bail shall not be required, nor excessive fines
imposed, nor cruel and unusual punishments inflicted."*
—8th Amendment to the U.S. Constitution

LONDON—1550 to 1750

It is the heyday of capital punishment in England.
During the reign of Henry VIII some 72,000 subjects will be
exterminated. But while the ranks of the condemned thin
rapidly over the next two hundred years, the list of crimes for
which an Englishman can be put to death is extended into
every nook and cranny of criminal justice. By 1750 the menu
of capital crimes covers some 200 offenses ranging from treason and murder to robbing a rabbit warren, cutting down a
tree, or marrying a Jew.

The methods are intended to impress—crucifixion,
drowning, impalement. People are boiled alive or burned at
the stake. They are hanged, beheaded or "drawn and quar-
tered"—a particularly involved piece of business that
includes a little of everything. The condemned man is
dragged through the streets to the place of execution where
he is hanged—but only until half-dead. Then, as he watches,
they slit open his abdomen, pull out his intestines and burn
them before his eyes so he can appreciate the full extent of
the Crown's wrath. When the prisoner loses interest, his
head is cut off and his body divided into more or less equal
parts for display.

The drawback to staging spectacular executions for
petty crimes like rabbit theft is that the common folk find it
distasteful and it ultimately becomes impossible to get a con-

viction. And that is the genius of the English jury system—a check valve on the natural authoritarian tendencies of the state. The Crown has little choice but to accommodate the shift in public opinion and over the next 80 years the list of capital offenses is down by half.[1]

The British colonials bring capital punishment to the New World in wide variations. In Virginia you might get the ax for stealing grapes, killing chickens or trading with the Indians, while New York colonists can be executed for striking their parents or denying the True God.[2]

In 1767 a young aristocrat from Milan named Cesare Beccaria electrifies the Age of Enlightenment with his essay, "On Crimes and Punishment." The immediate global impact of the work is astounding for the time. His fans include Katherine the Great, Voltaire, John Adams and Thomas Jefferson. Beccaria maintains that the state has no justification for taking a life. "Crimes are more effectually prevented by the *certainty* than the *severity* of punishment," he writes. "As punishments become more cruel, the minds of men... grow hardened and insensible," and in time, "the wheel terrifies no more than...the prison."[3]

Archduchess Maria Theresa is so impressed with this argument that the death penalty is abolished in Austria, and Thomas Jefferson of the colony of Virginia introduces a bill in the legislature to eliminate capital punishment for everything but murder and treason. It fails by a single vote. The argument over the definition of capital crimes will remain unsettled in the New World for the next two hundred years.

NEW YORK—1789

A glance at the sweep of history shows an inexorable trend toward moderation when it comes to official vengeance. From one century to the next, limiting the state's ability to do violence to its own citizens has become almost a barometer of human progress. By the time of the Constitutional Convention in Philadelphia nobody is suggesting that convicts be boiled alive, and the concept of forcing people to watch their guts go up in flames finds only minority support even among extremists.

When the First U.S. Congress assembles in Manhattan in 1789, the top item on the agenda is a collection of amendments to the new Constitution intended to nail down certain rights of the citizens. James Madison, one of the Constitution's leading architects, initially opposes the idea of tinkering with the work done in Philadelphia. He and his supporters insist that these rights are already implied in the existing document. But during the ratification process it has become clear that a lot of folks out there need reassurance. Thomas Jefferson, for one, says issues like freedom of speech and freedom of religion can't be left to the imagination. So Madison now takes the floor with a list of amendments of his own. He has come to the conclusion that the only way to sell this new government to the people is to lay out the safeguards in unequivocal terms—a "bill of rights."

For the men in this hall, the Eighth Amendment in particular is a reflection of recent personal experience with the excesses of the Crown. Many still bear the scars. The language they propose is simple and direct: "Excessive bail shall not be required, nor excessive fines imposed, nor cruel and unusual punishment inflicted."

There is little debate. Only a brief discussion about the meaning of "cruel and unusual," which is intentionally left unresolved because these men probably understand as clearly as anyone on the planet that the ground rules of society are subject to change without notice. They were born and bred loyal subjects of the English King. They meet here now as his equal.

But civilization, like evolution, advances incrementally. The first state to seriously limit the death penalty is Michigan in 1846, followed shortly by Rhode Island and Wisconsin. During the Civil War, opposition to capital punishment wanes as reformers focus on the anti-slavery movement. But the long term shift in public thinking about capital punishment seems inexorable. Before the end of the century several states have made the death penalty discretionary instead of mandatory. By the beginning of the First World War nine states have backed away from capital punishment and half a dozen have outlawed it altogether.[4]

Then almost overnight the country reverses engines. The chaos of wartime coupled with rapid industrialization leads to class conflicts that the establishment finds unnerving, especially in the wake of the Russian Revolution.

The anticipated violence from these conflicts does indeed materialize. But the driving force turns out not to be bearded Ukranian bomb throwers, but the 18th Amendment outlawing booze. From the onset of Prohibition in 1920, the murder rate doubles and then doubles again as the inevitable black market empires wage war over the staggering profits of illegal alcohol. The violence is all-pervasive. On one occasion there is a noon-time machine gun shootout right in front of the Standard Oil building in downtown Chicago. This routine mayhem is capped with the Crash of 1929, and an unparalleled jolt of fear ripples through the body politic. With socialists, anarchists and communists openly challenging the country's capitalist underpinnings, the death penalty suddenly seems more attractive. Most of the states that had canceled capital punishment at the turn of the century now have it back on the books and by the mid-1930s the number of executions is approaching an all-time high of 200 a year.

There will be more executions in the 1930s than any other decade in American history.

But where the First World War ramped up national anxiety, World War II has the opposite effect. Emerging from the conflict triumphant, the country has a sense of domestic security it hasn't seen in a lifetime. The popularity of the death penalty takes a nosedive and by the 1960s support for capital punishment has dropped from 70 percent to less than half.

Now the critics have the upper hand and their first target is the application of the death penalty to crimes other than murder—the question Jefferson raised in Virginia 200 years earlier. The primary issue is rape. Does the crime of rape, by itself, call for the punishment of death? The vast majority of these cases seem to involve black male defendants and white women but it is a white man who will bring the issue to a boil.

SAN QUENTIN—1960

Caryl Chessman is known as "the Red Light Bandit." Convicted in 1948 of kidnaping and rape, he terrified lover's lane in Los Angeles by posing as a cop and robbing the men and assaulting their girlfriends. Rape is a capital offense in California even if the victim isn't physically injured and Chessman has spent the last dozen years on death row. Seven times he has missed execution by a whisker.

Caryl Chessman breaks the mold. While he may look like a prizefighter with a busted nose, he has an I.Q. of 137 and he has not been idle in prison. Totally self-educated, he represents himself in court with an authority and command of the law that leaves the professionals open-mouthed. Maintaining his innocence, he has taken his case all the way to the Supreme Court no less than fifteen times. His first book—*Cell 2455 Death Row*—was a best-seller. Hollywood bought the rights and made the movie.

Chessman's notoriety has created an enormous political problem for California Governor Pat Brown, a liberal Democrat with an eye on the vice presidency. It's not so easy to execute an intellectual and Chessman's impending death has created a furor all over the world. Petitions by the sackful are arriving from France, Sweden, Italy, England, Mexico, Canada. The Vatican is appealing for clemency. So is Eleanor Roosevelt, Steve Allen, Dr. Albert Schweitzer, Aldous Huxley and the Queen of Belgium.

As the global champion of human rights, the United States now finds itself in the awkward position of defending the death penalty at a time when it is rapidly vanishing everywhere else. Europe in particular is turning away from capital punishment, partly as a result of Nazi atrocities and the two Great Wars that pulverized the Continent twice in one lifetime. They have seen enough killing.

Governor Brown, hard pressed from every side, tries to get rid of the ball with a lateral to the state legislature. He grants Chessman a stay of execution and calls a special session of the general assembly to "give the people of California, through the Legislature," a chance "to express themselves once more on capital punishment."[5]

It doesn't work. The Legislature refuses to get involved and they chuck the ball right back to Brown. A new date is set for the execution—Chessman's ninth.

With the governor's own son, Jerry, among the protestors outside the wall, Caryl Chessman is led into the octagonal green gas chamber at San Quentin a few minutes before 10:00 a.m. on Monday, May 2. He is strapped into one of the two steel chairs. Underneath his seat is a vial of acid and two cyanide pellets that will send him to oblivion. But the desperate last-minute battle to keep him alive, frantically pursued in state and federal court at every level over the last 72 hours, continues at this moment. Forty-five minutes ago the California Supreme Court voted 4-to-3 against a writ of habeas corpus. But Chessman's attorneys have just asked for a temporary stay to see if the U.S. Supreme Court will hear the motion.

Federal District Judge Louis E. Goodman thinks the idea has merit. At 10:03 he tells his assistant to connect him with the warden at San Quentin. In haste the secretary misdials. When she gets through minutes later the warden tells her that the cyanide pellets have just been dropped.[6]

PHILADELPHA—1963

Chessman's execution has put a face on death row that doesn't fit expectations and the wave of soul-searching that follows is about to merge with an even more powerful tide. The civil rights movement is starting to focus on criminal justice in the Old South and it's impossible to ignore the blatant racial disparity in capital punishment. Southern juries have been routinely dispatching black men to death row for raping white women, while the reverse—a white man raping a black woman—is treated much more sympathetically. In a case with both black and white co-defendants, the white man might get 20 years and the black man gets death.

For a knight errant fresh out of law school it is a heady moment to arrive on the scene and 28-year-old Anthony Amsterdam is more than equal to the occasion. Lean and hawk-like, the brilliant young attorney has just come from a stint at the Supreme Court as Justice Felix Frankfurter's law clerk, followed by a tour as an assistant U.S. Attorney for the District of Colombia.

Two days after returning to the University of

Pennsylvania Law School to teach at his alma mater he gets a call from Jack Greenberg, head of the Legal Defense Fund in New York. The LDF is a creation of the National Association for the Advancement of Colored People and it has become a powerful hammer on the anvil of justice. And now that young Tony Amsterdam has left government service, Jack Greenberg is offering him an opportunity to work for free. The LDF has several cases headed for the Supreme Court and they could use an insider's perspective. Amsterdam agrees to lend a hand and before long he's putting in 50 hours a week in addition to his full time teaching job. This will set the tone for his next thirty years.

Since there are few African-American lawyers anywhere in the south—Mississippi has three—the LDF is already representing most of the black death penalty defendants in Dixie and Amsterdam is quickly drawn into this urgent business. His analysis of the battlefield reveals plenty of room for maneuver. For one thing there is blatant racism throughout the process, everybody knows it, and all-white juries are just the most visible example. There are structural problems as well. In the typical death penalty trial the defendant's guilt and his sentence are usually decided at the same time. So the defendant has to choose between two constitutional rights. If he takes the Fifth and refuses to testify against himself, he forfeits his right to speak on his own behalf during sentencing.

Scouring the legal archives, the LDF team assembles a roster of potential lines of attack and it's immediately apparent that these arguments apply not just to individual cases but to whole categories of death row inmates. But before they can even consider the implications, events take the saddle and Amsterdam suddenly finds himself on the front lines.

In the summer of 1966 the State of Arkansas has six

men on death row facing imminent execution and three of them are represented by the LDF. Early in July, Governor Orval Faubus signs all six death warrants and blows town.

Within hours Amsterdam is on the phone dictating petitions and he manages to get stays for his clients in nothing flat. But the other three inmates don't even have lawyers. Amsterdam looks at Greenberg and says, "Can we let these guys die?"

Despite the fact that one of these defendants is white and therefore somewhat outside the normal concern of the LDF, they contact the astonished prisoners and offer to represent them. Amsterdam gets the federal district court to grant a stay for all six, but the judge puts them on a rush schedule. When he hears the petition of convicted rapist William L. Maxwell, he throws the case out of court and sets a new execution date. Maxwell is rescheduled to die on September 2, 1966. Amsterdam appeals to the Eighth Circuit federal court and they turn him down.

Two days before the execution, with the media now following each tack, Amsterdam takes the case to Supreme Court Justice Byron "Whizzer" White. At the last minute White grants a stay so the full court can review the petition. This decision gets enormous play because the questions raised by Amsterdam are constitutional and they go to the heart of the death penalty itself. In short order the LDF is inundated with calls from prisoners and their families, and from lawyers and law reformers all over the country.

Until the Maxwell case came along the LDF was saving people from the ax one at a time. Now it's clear they have in their hands the constitutional weapons for an attack that could lead to a rescue of death row inmates nationwide. "It's the equivalent of walking past somebody bleeding to death in a gutter," says Amsterdam, "and you have a tourniquet and you're not gonna use it."

On the other hand it is a staggering burden. They are a mere handful of lawyers, they're already stretched to the wire, and now they're about to announce that if any death penalty defendant anywhere in the country can't get competent counsel, the LDF will ride to the rescue. The situation calls for an army of volunteers, but raw recruits aren't likely to have capital trial experience. Since one of the issues is assembly-line justice they decide to counter with an assembly-line defense. Their solution would come to be known as the "Last Aid Kits."

The arguments at hand are rooted in the U.S. Constitution so it's possible to assemble a single pile of documents that will work anywhere in the country. Sifting all previous cases for the best reasoning, they put together a package of finely tooled petitions and start shipping them free of charge wherever they're requested. These prefabricated pleadings prove enormously successful. A lawyer anywhere, no matter how inexperienced, can fill in the blanks and in 15 minutes present the court with a brief that's probably more sophisticated than anything they've ever seen. If the judge denies relief, all the attorney has to do is pull out the next set of papers and move on.

By the end of the 1960s this rolling legal barrage has effectively brought the death penalty process in the U.S. to a grinding halt. There has not been an execution anywhere in the country since Colorado killed Louis Monge in 1967, and the number of prisoners waiting on death row is rising dramatically. Death penalty opponents now believe this fact alone could box in the U.S. Supreme Court. With over 600 inmates ready for execution, the high court will either have to rule against the death penalty or face a revolting nationwide bloodbath.

At this moment a Miami lawyer named Toby Simon kicks over the card table. Simon, a quirky, creative, sometime associate of the LDF, decides to take the "Last Aid" concept a step further. He files a class action lawsuit in Florida on behalf of the state's whole death row. Then he tosses the case to Amsterdam and Greenberg and says, "it's your baby now."[7]

Nobody has ever seen anything like it. When Amsterdam appears before the Florida Supreme Court, the state's attorney is dismayed. "This isn't a habeas corpus," he says, "it's a *habeas corpi*. Who ever heard of that?" But in this climate of uncertainty the momentum is with the reformers and the Florida high court decides to halt all executions until the federal judiciary deals with the underlying issues.

WASHINGTON D.C.—JUNE 5, 1971

For years the U.S. Supreme Court has managed to dodge fundamental questions about the death penalty by focusing on the details. Just last month they denied relief to a couple of inmates who appealed on procedural grounds, but the Legal Defense Fund simply whipped out the next round of challenges and won a stay. And since there are plenty more challenges where those came from, it's clear that the justices can no longer ignore the elephant in the courtroom. Their in-box now contains 120 death penalty appeals.

With the end of the current term fast approaching, the Court announces that it will hear arguments on the constitutionality of capital punishment in the next session. Three cases covering a range of issues have been consolidated into a single question: "Does the imposition and carrying out of the death penalty in this case constitute cruel and unusual punishment in violation of the Eighth and Fourteenth Amendments?" The case is named for Henry Furman, a defendant represented by Amsterdam. *Furman v. Georgia* is the case the LDF has been waiting for.[8]

But before Amsterdam can start prepping he gets an urgent call from the West Coast. A group of young lawyers headed by Berkeley attorney Jerry Falk wants the LDF to run those Florida arguments past the California Supreme Court. The issues are almost identical and California has a "cruel and unusual punishment" prohibition just like the 8th Amendment. It would, in a sense, be the perfect warm-up for the coming duel in Washington. Without a break in stride Amsterdam and his anti-death squad head for the Coast.

The day before the case is to be heard in Los Angeles, Jerry Falk picks Amsterdam up at Stanford for the drive south. Rolling down Highway 101 Amsterdam is rehearsing the arguments in his head but all Falk wants to talk about is the pair of brand new skis that were stolen off the roof of his car up at Lake Tahoe last weekend. He's raving on and on until Amsterdam finally tells him to shut up so he can concentrate. Falk tries to contain himself but he just can't get over it.

The next morning they walk in to face the seven justices of the California Supreme Court before a packed house. The atmosphere is crackling. This court has already refused to hold the death penalty unconstitutional on several occasions. Now it's up to Amsterdam to bring the mountain to Mohammed.

Five minutes into his opening argument he's interrupted by the Chief Justice. "Mr. Amsterdam," says the judge, "is there *any* crime for which you could imagine the death penalty would be acceptable?"

Amsterdam hesitates, trying to avoid some unforseen pitfall. Jerry Falk slides a note across the table. It says: "SKI THEFT."

Clenching his jaw, Amsterdam somehow manages to choke down a convulsion of laughter—and the impulse to strangle Falk—and goes on to deliver a presentation that moves six of the seven jurists to agree with their colleagues in the Sunshine State. In deciding that the death penalty "degrades and dehumanizes all who participate in its processes," the California Supreme Court goes Florida one better. They empty death row in a single sweep. Five women and 102 men simultaneously have their sentences commuted to life in prison.[9] A de facto moratorium now exists on both coasts.

WASHINGTON, D.C.—1972

For the past four years no one has been executed in the United States. Every jurisdiction is on hold waiting to see what the High Court will do. Once again it's up to the LDF. In a chilly January wind, Tony Amsterdam, Jack Greenberg, and LDF strategist Michael Meltsner mount the broad steps of the Corinthian temple that hosts the nine most powerful philosophers on earth. As Amsterdam enters through the great bronze doors he feels the full weight of history. The last time the Legal Defense Fund attorneys marched down this corridor on a mission of such moment was when Thurgood Marshall argued *Brown v. Board of Education*. Now Thurgood Marshall sits on the bench.

On the other hand some of the court's friendlier faces have been replaced. The near-simultaneous retirement of four justices from the Warren court, including the Chief Justice himself, has given President Nixon a remarkable opportunity to shift the balance of power and he has taken full advantage of it. Warren Burger, the new Chief Justice, heads a court steering rapidly to the right.

As Amsterdam enters the great chamber he finds it

jammed to the walls just as in California. He glances toward the alcove where he and his fellow law clerks used to peek through the curtains and he sees the curtains have been pulled back and extra rows of seats have been added. All the clerks are here.

Opposing Amsterdam is Charles Alan Wright, one of the country's foremost legal scholars—and something of a surprise in the role of death penalty defender. Most people think of Wright as a liberal. A professor at the University of Texas, he is the leading authority on U.S. civil and criminal procedure and there is a rumor that Chief Justice Warren Burger personally sought him out to present the pro-death penalty argument. Wright denies it.

In this extraordinary face-off between two preeminent law professors the dialogue is civil enough at first—somebody likens it to a faculty meeting. But the issues are hardly academic and Amsterdam's life-and-death urgency dominates the courtroom. His command of the facts is legendary. When a judge once told him that a case was not on the page he cited, Amsterdam shot back that the judge's volume must be misbound. It was.[10]

In a wide-ranging assault Amsterdam argues that only a tiny percentage of potential capital defendants are sentenced to death. When a country of 200 million people inflicts such severe punishment only a few dozen times a year, it's almost certainly being applied arbitrarily. Like lightning, it strikes practically at random. The only consistent pattern is that it strikes with a distinct preference for non-whites.

Amsterdam's argument is interrupted several times by the Chief Justice who seems to be almost baiting him. It's nothing personal—their relationship goes back to the days when Burger was on the D.C. Circuit Court—but on this issue they are poles apart. At one point the Chief Justice asks,

"If the courts undertook to accept your concept of 'cruel and unusual'...couldn't the court make exceptions?"

Two words leap to Amsterdam's mind: "SKI THEFT."

Again he manages to recover. "If Your Honor means, could the court find the death penalty is unconstitutional for some crimes and not for others," he says, "I do not believe it should or can..."

By the time he and his colleagues make their way back through the bronze doors and down the steps everyone's congratulating him on a powerful performance.

WASHINGTON—JUNE 29, 1972

> *"The Court holds that the imposition and carrying out of the death penalty in these cases constitute cruel and unusual punishment in violation of the Eighth and Fourteenth Amendments. The judgment in each case is therefore reversed.... and the cases are remanded for further proceedings."*

In the matter of *Furman v. Georgia* (408 US 238) the results are exactly what the opponents of capital punishment dreamed of. The death penalty in the United States is now officially unconstitutional—not only under the Eighth Amendment as cruel and unusual, but under the Fourteenth as well because it fails the test of "due process of law." But the verdict is physically enormous as well—over 200 pages—and ominously, every single justice has written a separate opinion. As Amsterdam races through the document he realizes it contains a ticking bomb.

To begin with, all four of the new Nixon appointees—Burger, Blackmun, Powell and Rehnquist—were against it. A single vote could tilt everything the other way. And of the five justices who voted with the majority, only three of them say unequivocally that the death penalty is unconstitutional. Potter Stewart and Byron White will agree only that it is cruel and unusual *as now applied*. Which means they think it might be fixable.

Nonetheless it's hard to focus on anything other than the triumph at the finish line of this grueling marathon. But Amsterdam knows the death penalty supporters are enraged over the way they were outmaneuvered and he fully expects some kind of a backlash.[11]

He has no idea.

CALIFORNIA—1973

Since all prisoners currently on death row got there under a system now considered cruel and unusual, *Furman v. Georgia* has the practical effect of canceling every death sentence in the country. Unfortunately for the proponents of reform, three of the 600 prisoners who escape the noose are poster boys for capital punishment: Sirhan Sirhan who changed history all by himself with the assassination of Robert Kennedy, Richard Speck who slaughtered eight young nurses in Chicago, and Charlie Manson, the Devil incarnate.

In truth, there is not the slightest chance that any of these lunatics will ever breathe free air again—Speck's death sentence for example was commuted to 1200 years—but a life sentence under current law does not rule out the possibility of parole. This loophole will soon be closed in many states with provisions for "life without possibility of parole" but too late for Manson, Sirhan and Speck. So every few years the public will be treated to the image of, say, Charlie Manson with a swastika on his forehead, swearing that if we'll only let him out he'll eat us alive. And then authorities in Illinois discover that Richard Speck, apparently a celebrity down in Stateville, is having prostitutes and drugs delivered by the guards. When a secret video of this romp shows up on the nightly news it would be hard to imagine a better TV spot for capital punishment.

WASHINGTON—1976

Once again the country is undergoing a postwar transformation and this one's not nearly as pretty as the last one. Where World War II welded the country together in lockstep, Vietnam splits it down the middle. And now the country is in the throes of a stunning cultural transformation as women almost overnight begin shrugging off centuries of second-class citizenship. The epoch that began under the banner of Peace and Love ends in Watts with the SLA shootout after a decade of riots, fire and chaos.

Like a schooner working to windward, the Ship of State puts helm alee. Now the wind is once more with the death penalty supporters. A 1976 Gallup Poll shows public support for capital punishment has jumped 25 percent in the last decade.[12]

Six months after the Supreme Court declares the death penalty unconstitutional the legislatures in 35 states are already crafting new statutes designed to win over at least one more Supreme Court justice. The two swing votes, Potter Stewart and Byron White, said in *Furman* that capital punishment cannot be left to the whim of the jury. To get over this hurdle the penalty would somehow have to be applied without discrimination in some logical fashion.

During the high court's 1976 session, several states try to get through the wicket by eliminating any hint of discrimination by reviving mandatory death sentences—everybody goes. But this one-size-fits-all method completely ignores the mitigating circumstances that may exist in indi-

vidual cases and the majority won't go for it. Finally the State
of Georgia cracks the code in a case called *Gregg v. Georgia.*
In addition to spelling out specific guidelines for judge and
jury about when death may be imposed, the Georgia law provides for a split trial—one phase to determine guilt or innocence with a separate trial for the penalty. The law also stip-
ulates an automatic appeal so that every case will be
reviewed by a higher court to make sure the sentence isn't
out of line.

Gregg v. Georgia is the key that reopens death row. Both
Potter Stewart and Byron White are satisfied that the so-
called bifurcated trial with jury guidelines and an automatic
appeal will do the trick. Justice Douglas, the court's most liberal member, has been replaced by John Paul Stevens who
votes with the majority in a 7-to-2 triumph for the death
penalty supporters. Other states immediately pick up the cue
and begin crafting similar laws.

Tony Amsterdam and his colleagues are stunned. "We
expected that there would be some attempt to get around
Furman," he says, "but the magnitude and immediacy of it
was really quite surprising."[13]

With the Supreme Court now hostile territory, the LDF
has no choice but to revert to guerrilla warfare. At a strategy session immediately following the *Gregg* decision,
Amsterdam lays out the battle plan, an ingenious scheme to
trap the opposition in a Catch-22. If a death penalty statute
is not precise in its instructions, they will attack it as granting prosecutors and jurors too much discretion. And if it is
precise, they will attack it for unconstitutionally preventing
individualized sentencing![14]

This deft maneuver leads to 14 wins out of the first 15
cases but these victories are not without cost. The LDF and
their allies are successfully throwing sand in the gears of the

death penalty machine but their opponents—already steaming—are enraged by this blatant manipulation of the criminal justice system. They resolve to engage in a little blatant manipulation of their own. And so the stage is set for a contorted and destructive legal dance that seems almost designed to make everything worse.

William Rehnquist, who will be appointed Chief Justice in 1986, has held a hard-line position on capital punishment since his youth. Back in the 1950s when atom-spies Julius and Ethel Rosenberg were facing the electric chair, Rehnquist was clerking for Justice Robert Jackson and he wrote a memo saying, "It is too bad that drawing and quartering has been abolished."[15]

With this level of philosophical commitment to retribution it's easy to understand why the LDF's obstructionist game is driving Justice Rehnquist and his fellow death penalty advocates up the wall. Rehnquist decides to counter with an equally ingenious strategy of his own. He will abolish the federal writ of habeas corpus through judicial fiat. In 1977 he writes an opinion that makes it virtually impossible to raise any of the 90-odd possible constitutional claims in federal court unless the defendant's attorney made these specific objections *during the original trial*.[16] This basically guts Amsterdam's strategy. The LDF has been relying on a sophisticated analysis of the case record after the fact. Now the only objections that count are the ones raised during the trial. There is no way the average lawyer can have this vast assortment of constitutional claims at the tip of his tongue.[17]

Nevertheless, the LDF blocking game manages to hold the line for a time. In the five years after *Gregg*, sixty percent of the death sentences are reversed.[18] But like Chinese water torture, the endless parade of defense obstructions is cranking up the tension. During a death penalty argument in 1981, Justice Rehnquist complains that the inmate's repeated appeals have cost the state a fortune. Thurgood Marshall fires back, "It would have been cheaper to shoot him right after he was arrested, wouldn't it?"

WASHINGTON—APRIL, 1987

David Baldus is a professor of law at the University of Iowa and he and his associates have spent the last several years on a massive study of 2400 Georgia murder cases from the mid-1970s, the period immediately after capital punishment was reestablished. The results are quite unequivocal about who gets death in the Peach Tree state:

Black Defendant/White Victim	22%
White Defendant/White Victim	8%
White Defendant/Black Victim	3%
Black Defendant/Black Victim	1%

The Baldus study is the latest battering ram assembled by the death penalty foes and it is the centerpiece of the most formidable attack on capital punishment since *Furman*.[19] The evidence clearly shows that capital punishment, despite all the brand new safeguards, is still being handed out on a racial basis. This, say the abolitionists, means the death penalty is essentially un-fixable and must be done away with altogether.

Justice Harry Blackmun happens to have a background in mathematics and when he examines the Baldus study he finds it quite compelling.[20] The researchers have taken into account some 230 variables in a sophisticated statistical analysis and no matter which way they slice it the death penalty comes out racially tilted. Justice William Brennan calls it, "the most sophisticated capital sentencing analysis ever performed."[21]

The case in which this study is presented to the Supreme Court involves Warren McCleskey, a black man convicted of killing a police officer during a furniture store holdup. He claims he was unconstitutionally sentenced to death for racial reasons: his victim was white, he's black. The Baldus study seems to prove his point.

Years later political scientist Dennis Dorin, digging through the personal papers of Justice Thurgood Marshall, will come across a startling memo from Justice Antonin Scalia written as this decision was being hammered out.[22] Scalia, a freshman on the Court, warns his fellow jurists that the Baldus study is probably correct—Georgia's capital sentencing is racist—but it doesn't matter. While McCleskey's sentence may have been racially motivated, there's nothing the Supreme Court can do about it because America is a racist society and disparities like this are inevitable.[23]

This is a line of reasoning the Court hasn't seen since 1896 when *Plessy v. Ferguson* legitimized segregation in holding that "If one race be inferior to the other socially, the constitution of the United States cannot put them upon the same plane."[24]

Whatever else it may be, the Scalia memo is a high water mark for pragmatism in American jurisprudence, and his private sensibilities are reflected in the final decision. In a remarkable change of course on the issue of race, the Supreme Court decides that this time the numbers don't matter. The sharply divided opinion rules that even though the end result of Georgia's new capital punishment system may be racially biased overall, McCleskey has failed to prove that this particular judge, jury or prosecutor in this case was specifically biased against him. Using this yardstick McCleskey would almost have to get a signed confession from the governor admitting that they gave him death because of his skin color.

The opinion's sweat-stained reasoning gives way to a flash of clarity at the end. Writing for the majority, Justice Lewis Powell, Jr. says, "McCleskey's claim, taken to its logical conclusion, throws into serious question the principles that underlie our entire criminal justice system... [I]f we accepted McCleskey's claim that racial bias has impermissibly tainted the capital sentencing decision, we could soon be faced with similar claims as to other types of penalty."[25]

Justice William Brennan strips the cloak of gentility from Powell's argument with a single slash. He calls it, "fear of too much justice."[26]

"At some point in this case," writes Brennan, "Warren McCleskey doubtless asked his lawyer whether a jury was likely to sentence him to die. A candid reply to this question would have been disturbing. First, counsel would have to tell McCleskey that few of the details of the crime or of McCleskey's past criminal conduct were more important than the fact that his victim was white..."[27]

Brennan's withering dissent ends with a warning. "It is tempting to pretend that minorities on death row share a fate in no way connected to our own, that our treatment of them sounds no echoes beyond the chambers in which they die. Such an illusion is ultimately corrosive, for the reverberations of injustice are not so easily confined."[28]

CALIFORNIA—APRIL, 1992

Although the death penalty machinery is once again in motion it is creaking at every joint. Despite all attempts to lubricate the gears, the number of people sentenced to death every year still far exceeds the number of executions and the death row pileup is again growing dramatically. The appeals for this burgeoning army of prisoners are being handled by a new generation of death penalty attorneys, often men and women who got jump-started by the LDF or the ACLU, and they are dedicated, obsessed, and endlessly inventive. It's not unusual for them to see their clients through the appellate system six, eight, ten times, testing every conceivable avenue of escape. For this monastic corps of attorneys—often working to exhaustion for little or no money—this is a holy mission. They have seen the death penalty, they are convinced it is evil, and they are determined to stop it. Since the issue is actually life and death there is no approach too extreme if it has the slightest hope of delaying the ax. As long as the client is still breathing there's a chance.

In warfare we often tend to imitate our adversaries' most despised qualities and the Supreme Court is unable to resist. The new conservative majority responds to the LDF assault with an obsession of their own—greasing the skids for the prisoners on death row.

Those Americans who support the death penalty—almost 80 percent of the electorate in 1990—are disgusted by these interminable delays and Chief Justice William Rehnquist is infuriated. Rehnquist, who used to be alone in his visceral support for capital punishment, now has two equally committed allies in Antonin Scalia and Clarence Thomas. Together they form the nucleus of the majority and their increasing frustration with the likes of Anthony Amsterdam, Dick Burr, Stephen Bright and their acolytes is driving them crazy. From the tone of the opinions in this era you can almost hear their teeth grinding. As Justice Powell complains in *Woodward v. Hutchins*, "This is another capital case in which a last-minute application for a stay of execution and a new petition for habeas corpus relief have been filed with no explanation as to why the claims were not raised earlier..."[29]

From the Congressional Cloak Room to the neighborhood saloon there is pressure on the courts to speed things up. The average citizen finds it incredible that someone sentenced to death for a heinous crime can still be breathing a dozen years later. The man who will finally snap the issue into focus is Robert Alton Harris, a drifter who killed two teenage boys because he wanted their pickup truck.

Harris is the first person scheduled for execution in the California gas chamber in 32 years and his impending death has become symbolic for all sides. The last man to be strapped in that steel capsule was Caryl Chessman.

Harris's attorneys have artfully dodged this moment for thirteen years. Four times they've saved him and they are frantically trying to pull it out of the hat one more time. During the final twelve hours they manage to get the Ninth Circuit Court of Appeals to issue three separate stays. But the Supreme Court is standing by in Washington and they immediately lift each stay in turn. At 3:30 a.m. Harris is strapped into the chair that sent Chessman to oblivion—but before the pellets can drop another Ninth Circuit federal judge issues a stay.

Harris's current petition has nothing to do with guilt or innocence. He's attacking the method of execution—lethal gas—as cruel and unusual because it inflicts needless suffering. There's plenty of evidence for this—and in fact the courts will later force California to get rid of the gas chamber—but this complaint pushes Rehnquist and his allies over the edge. If Robert Alton Harris was so concerned about lethal gas, why did he wait twelve years to bring it up?

When the Justices went to sleep last night, Harris was on his way into the death chamber. Now they wake up and discover he's back in his cell. Fuming, they lift the fourth stay and then issue an astounding order: "No further stays of Robert Alton Harris's execution shall be entered by the federal courts except upon order of this Court."

Perhaps they had no choice. It was beginning to look like the only way to kill Harris was to drive a stake through his heart by the light of the moon, and this injunction sweeps all arguments off the table. The condemned man is led once more into the gas chamber. But draconian remedies are not without cost. Handed down almost as a royal edict, the High Court is saying in effect that the twenty-eight federal judges of the Ninth Circuit can't be trusted.

Since the Court's action is arguably unconstitutional, reaction is swift and acidic. Most of the country's legal scholars are dismayed and many are outraged. One Ninth Circuit judge calls it "treason to the Constitution."[30]

The Supreme Court apparently underestimated the task they had set for themselves when they reinstated capital punishment. They now find themselves in the business of death penalty administration for 38 different jurisdictions and the legal structures they are erecting are becoming more complex and paradoxical with every decision.[31] The Rehnquist majority is philosophically inclined to leave the states to their own devices whenever possible, but with the Court now committed to expediting the execution process, this laissez-faire approach is about to yield some mind-boggling results.

WASHINGTON—JANUARY, 1993

It's been ten years since Leonel Torres Herrera was convicted of killing two police officers and sentenced to death. After fully exhausting all avenues in the Texas state courts and taking a habeas corpus petition all the way to the top, he is, not surprisingly, back again at the eleventh hour. But this time Herrera has some new evidence. It indicates that he's innocent. Four witnesses have filed affidavits complete with positive polygraph results saying that it was Herrera's brother—now deceased—who fired the shots. Among the affidavits is a sworn statement from a former Texas state judge who independently examined the evidence and says Herrera is not the man. His attorneys argue that executing a person for a crime he did not commit is a violation of the Eighth Amendment's prohibition against cruel and unusual punishment.

In a triumph of form over content, the Supreme Court rules 6-to-3 that they are not required to hear evidence of Leonel Herrera's innocence. Under Texas law, post-conviction evidence must be filed within thirty days of the end of the trial. Unfortunately for Herrera, the evidence that might have saved him wasn't available until eight years after the trial. But the salient fact is, he's too late. He missed the 30-day deadline.

As Chief Justice William Rehnquist explains, "we cannot say that Texas's refusal to entertain petitioner's newly discovered evidence eight years after his conviction transgresses a principle of fundamental fairness." Or to put it in layman's terms: all of the legal requirements for Leonel Herrera's execution have been met by the State of Texas and the fact that he might be innocent is none of our business.

Rehnquist and his colleagues are not totally unsympathetic. They point out to Herrera that he has an appropriate remedy for his quandary at the state level. They urge him to seek executive clemency. And thus the High Court, historically the nation's last refuge from the lynch mob, washes their hands of the matter and passes the baton to the Governor of

Texas. A few weeks later Herrera's appeal for executive clemency is denied and he is executed on May 12.[32]

WASHINGTON—1994

There is an inherent structural conflict between the right of the accused to a fair trial and the demands of the state for swift and certain punishment. Now that the Supreme Court has decided to weigh in on the swift-and-certain side of the argument the mental gymnastics required to support some of these decisions seem to be taking a toll.

Just before retirement, Justice Harry Blackmun writes in one of his final opinions: "From this day forward, I no longer shall tinker with the machinery of death...Rather than continue to coddle the Court's delusion that the desired level of fairness has been achieved...I feel morally and intellectually obligated simply to concede that the death penalty experiment has failed."[33]

A few months later Justice Lewis Powell Jr., now retired as well, was asked by his biographer whether he would change any of his votes. *McCleskey v. Kemp* was at the top of his list. What's more, he said that he would now vote against the death penalty in any case. If Justice Powell had come to that conclusion when it mattered, *McCleskey* would have been affirmed and the whole process of capital litigation would have taken a profoundly different course.

OKLAHOMA CITY—APRIL, 1995

Despite all efforts by the Rehnquist court to clear the roadblocks, there are now some 3054 prisoners awaiting death in the U.S. and their ranks are increasing at the rate of 150 a year. Clearly this isn't working. On Capitol Hill, Republicans and Democrats alike are scrambling to figure out some way to break the log-jam. In situations like this it sometimes takes a dramatic event to move Congress one way or the other but nobody is prepared for the catastrophe in Oklahoma City.

On April 19 a truck bomb explodes in front of the Murrah Federal Building and 168 people die in the blast, many of them children at the onsite day-care center. It is one of the most devastating terrorist acts ever on U.S. soil. When it turns out the culprit is not the expected Arab militant, but one of our own—and a decorated war veteran to boot—it's a blow to the solar plexus.

The front-page picture of the bloody infant cradled in the fireman's arms is galvanic. If the perpetrator of this horror could be turned over to the mob at this instant there would be nothing left to discuss. As soon as Timothy McVeigh is identified there are demands for his head and by the time he emerges from the jailhouse in his orange jumpsuit he is surrounded by a platoon of lawmen for good reason. The crowd would have ripped him to pieces.

But while the prosecution is certain to demand death, everybody knows that under the present system McVeigh could well wind up sitting around watching TV ten or fifteen years from now. The Supreme Court majority has done everything they can but their efforts are continually thwarted by that army of clever defense attorneys. Something has to be done and Congress is ready. The result is a stunning piece of legislation that sets back the clock on prisoners' rights by some 700 years.

Known as the Anti-terrorism and Effective Death Penalty Act, it's an attempt to simplify the capital punishment process by reigning in the federal judiciary and getting them off the backs of the state courts.[34] The objective is to try to cut the time between sentence and execution down to a reasonable time frame. In their zeal to do battle with the obstructionist defense attorneys they find they must set aside a fundamental right that dates to the Magna Carta.

When King John knuckled under to his own noblemen at Runnymede, the document he signed contained a clause saying, "no freemen shall be taken or imprisoned...or exiled or in any way destroyed...except by the lawful judgement of his peers or by the law of the land." Through the ages this concept has come to mean that a judge can confront the king's men at any moment and demand to see the prisoner to make sure he's being held lawfully and not on some royal whim. Over the last seven centuries, it has evolved into a central pillar of common law known as The Great Writ—in Latin, *habeas corpus*—"produce the body."

The U.S. Constitution guarantees the writ "shall not be suspended, unless when in cases of rebellion or invasion the public safety may require it." During the civil rights movement, the writ allowed federal judges to save people like the Reverend Martin Luther King from the clutches of southern justice. In the death penalty arena it has been the ultimate lifeline for a prisoner being railroaded to the gallows by a state court gone mad. It insured that justice would be more or less equal from coast to coast.

The new law installs a ticking clock. Following the example of Texas, the Great Writ is still available to the condemned prisoner, but only for six months. After that, any new evidence he or she may discover is irrelevant because this train is moving on. The *New York Times* calls it "the most rigorous constraint on the constitutional right to seek Federal review of convictions since Lincoln suspended the writ of habeas corpus in the Civil War."[35]

For death penalty supporters this is a moment of heady triumph, but as with Tony Amsterdam's countervailing victory 24 years before, the celebration is premature—disrupted almost immediately by an assault from a totally unexpected quarter.

CALIFORNIA HIGHWAY 128—SPRING, 1983

The road to Navarro Head on the coast south of Ft. Bragg is a thin ribbon winding over oak-covered hillsides through the wine country of Mendocino County. Since Kary Mullis could probably drive this highway with his eyes closed, he's lost in thought tonight as his girlfriend sleeps in the seat beside him. In his mind's eye, he's able to visualize the double helix of deoxyribonucleic acid—the key to life— almost as if he could touch it. At the Silicone Valley lab where he and his girlfriend spend their weekdays, Mullis is struggling with a new computer program that he hopes will help analyze the DNA molecule.

The discovery of DNA in 1953 was a technological earthquake that reverberated through almost every other field of science. In addition to triggering a tidal wave of innovation in medicine, it is revolutionizing the criminal justice system because DNA can identify any individual on the planet. Unfortunately the technology is still crude and the tests require a large sample of blood or tissue to be conclusive. Theoretically, a single molecule should be enough for a comparison because that's the point of DNA—it's replicated identically in every cell in the body. And since each one carries our whole blueprint...

All of a sudden Mullis takes his foot off the accelerator. He coasts to a stop at the edge of the road and stares into the night. Then he grabs pad and pencil and flips on the map light. He just realized that the whole point of DNA—replication—could be put to work using a single piece as a pattern—and you could reproduce as much as you want. Take a lone DNA fragment, add the right chemicals in the right sequence, and that fragment will do what it's supposed to do: make copies of itself. And since each copy can make copies, the process is exponential—2, 4, 8, 16, 32—and 25 steps later you have a billion copies.

Mullis's midnight leap will be known as polymerase chain reaction and "PCR" will win him the Nobel Prize for Chemistry. It will also transform the criminal justice system in a quite amazing way, for the new technique means a microscopic dot of dried blood or tissue can now be linked to a single human being. For law enforcement, this is the biggest news since fingerprints.[36]

NEW YORK—1992

Barry Scheck and Peter Neufeld, a couple of former public defenders from the South Bronx, are among the first lawyers in the U.S. to grasp the significance of DNA matching. "We realized that this is a remarkable tool," says Scheck. "You could go back and look at the evidence 10, 20, 30 years later." In the early 1990s they are drawn into the cause of a Long Island truck driver who's halfway through a 20-year sentence for rape. Using a science that didn't exist when the man went to prison, they established that his DNA does not match the sperm sample in evidence at the trial. Nine months later when the judge finally tells the fellow he is free to go, it is a matter of hours before word ricochets through the country's whole prison system. Scheck and Neufeld are immediately inundated with letters and phone calls.

To handle the flow, they establish a clinical program at Cardozo Law School called the Innocence Project to help inmates who are challenging convictions based on DNA testing. With an impressive army of volunteers they begin reopening files all over the country where the DNA evidence still exists, and out of the first sixty cases, half are reversed or overturned.[37]

Nobody ever expected the system to be perfect but this is ridiculous. Every month now there is another astounding image of an innocent man walking off death row. The Innocence Project is currently handling over a hundred cases with a thousand more waiting in line. Scheck and Neufeld say this is only the tip of the iceberg.

Their bleak assessment may turn out to be an understatement. The revelations now being extracted from the all-knowing DNA will in time save scores of innocent citizens from prison and death row. But for a host of prosecutors, police officers and judges out across the land who have managed over the years to convict people on bogus evidence, the tale of the double helix is about to become a living nightmare.

> *"The technology... happened to become available before the physical evidence from the crime was lost or destroyed...It is anybody's guess how many other innocent prisoners have not had the benefit of this sort of luck."*
>
> —Samuel R. Gross, Professor of Law, University of Michigan.[38]

CHAPTER THREE

"No State shall...deny to any person within its jurisdiction the equal protection of the laws."
—14th Amendment to the U.S. Constitution

WHEATON, ILLINOIS—MAY, 1983

They call him "The Black Knight." Aggressive, single-minded, ruthless in combat, he has run up an enviable record as DuPage County's chief of criminal prosecutions. The local defense attorneys despise him and the feeling is mutual. He can't understand how some of these criminal lawyers can live with themselves. To keep them in check, Tom Knight has honed himself into an instrument of legal vengeance, and while he has plenty of enemies among the local barristers, he doesn't particularly give a damn.

There is, however, one trial attorney whose distaste for Knight is not so easily dismissed. Jim Ryan, who recently faced off with Knight in a nose-to-nose courtroom shouting match, is now running for DuPage County state's attorney. If he wins, Knight will be out on his ass.

The tension is heightened by the fact that Knight's boss, J. Michael Fitzsimmons, is a Republican maverick. Ryan, the Republican party stalwart, will probably get the backing of the local machine. The last time Ryan campaigned against Fitzsimmons in the Republican primary, Fitzsimmons squeaked by with a bare 300 votes.[1]

And there is a threatening cloud on the horizon. The Jeanine Nicarico case is dead in the water. If the little girl's killer isn't nailed pretty soon, the political consequences could be profound. DuPage County is white bread America and brutal murders of children do not happen here. Wheaton, the county seat, may be a mere twenty miles west of the Chicago Loop but it's light years from big city crime and violence. This is where Reverend Billy Graham chose to base his ministry. It's one of the few U.S. cities with a population over 50,000 where you can't buy a drink.

In a setting like this, violence of any kind is remarkable. But when a 10-year-old girl is dragged from her suburban ranch house in broad daylight and raped and sodomized and has her skull crushed, the effect is tectonic. Jeanine Nicarico was a bright, lively fifth grader just beginning to blossom. Her only sin was to catch the flu and stay home from school.

Imagine the chill when her mother, Patricia, came home and found the door jamb splintered, the front door kicked in, her daughter gone, and the girl's little dog cowering in the laundry room. Imagine the shudder that rocked the whole county two days later when her body was found along a hiking trail with her "Snow White" nightie pulled up over her head. Every parent in the western suburbs must have felt the change in climate. Suddenly the monster under the bed was no joke. Here was the bogeyman come to life.

The FBI was involved in the beginning but after a month and a half of dead-end leads they bailed in mid-April, leaving the case to local law enforcement. Jeanine was snatched on February 25 and now, nine weeks later, all that Sheriff Richard Doria's detectives have to show for their efforts is a pair of local Latinos who may or may not know something.

Knight, however, can no longer sit on his hands and await developments. He has assured Jeanine's parents that justice will be done and he intends to deliver. As lead prosecutor for DuPage County, he has awesome resources at his fingertips and it's time to exercise them. Early in May he con-

venes a special grand jury. It's an unusual move—a grand jury
normally gets the case *after* the evidence is assembled—but
these are unusual times. Grand juries have subpoena power,
which means Knight doesn't have to wait for the sheriff.
Now he can run his own investigation. He can arrest people
and force them to testify under oath, and if they don't come
through he can threaten them with indictment.[2]

On May 12, 1983, Knight kicks off his personal probe
with a parade of witnesses, and early in the lineup are the two
Latinos—Rolando Cruz and Alex Hernandez—a couple of
petty thieves from the nearby industrial river town of Aurora.
These mopes barely knew each other but they came to the
attention of the authorities when they separately told the
cops they might know something about the case. Their leads
went nowhere but Knight believes that if he puts them on
the hot seat he may be able to sweat something out of them
that the detectives could not.

The detectives themselves are skeptical. John Sam is a
graying veteran of the DuPage County Sheriff's office and a
top-flight pro by all accounts. He leads the unit in felony
arrests, all accomplished through solid investigative police
work without flash, dash or gunplay. He thinks Knight is
jumping the gun with his premature grand jury investigation. Besides, the "informants" in this instance are not very
convincing. Alex Hernandez, for example, has an I.Q. of
around 65 and he's a notorious liar. Nineteen, unemployed
and virtually homeless, his statements are inherently contradictory, he can't keep anything straight, and he has no
information that hasn't already been on the nightly news.
There's now a $10,000 reward for Jeanine Nicarico's killer.
Sam figures the stupid punk is just trying to make a buck off
somebody else's misery.[3]

He's got the same opinion of Rolando Cruz. Cruz may

have a slightly sharper wit but he's equally carefree with the facts. He called the cops to tell them he'd been threatened by Hernandez and when they brought him into the station he said he'd heard that Hernandez and a couple of other guys had killed Jeanine at a violent orgy and dumped her body later. Unfortunately there is not a single detail of his version that matches the physical evidence. Jeanine had been killed at or near where she was found, Sam is certain of that, and the apartment that Cruz fingered as the death scene was clean as a whistle. "I thought Cruz was just a bullshitting asshole the first time I met him," said Sam. "That, and someone looking for a free ride."[4]

Tom Knight, however, is coming around to the idea that Cruz and Hernandez not only know more than they're telling, but that they might actually have been involved. Maybe the little girl's death was the result of a botched burglary. It was a school day, right? There wasn't supposed to be anybody home. Jeanine surprised them and they killed her.

The problem with this theory as far as John Sam is concerned is that it flies in the face of logic and experience. Jeanine Nicarico was sexually assaulted. Burglars don't grab a little girl and leave everything in the house untouched. True, a couple of burglars taken by surprise might panic and kill a witness but they wouldn't assault her first. The FBI psychological profilers have already established that a sex crime like this is committed on purpose, not as an afterthought. They say the killer was a loner who had some major blowout in his personal life just prior to the crime.

WHEATON—SEPTEMBER, 1983

Rolando Cruz and Alex Hernandez are not the only targets in the D.A.'s crosshairs. Stephen Buckley, a white 20-year-old unemployed dope smoker with a minor beef for breaking and entering was one of the first suspects the police brought in. After a brutal interrogation, Detective John Sam gave him a pass. But Tom Knight did not. Knight is convinced that Stephen Buckley's boot kicked in Jeanine Nicarico's front door. Unfortunately he's having trouble convincing the experts. The DuPage County crime lab refuses to say that the boot prints match, so Knight sends Buckley's boot print to the state police crime lab in Springfield. When they refuse to confirm the match, he takes it to the Kansas Bureau of Investigation. They say the same thing. As a last resort, Knight sends it to Professor Louise Robbins, an anthropologist from the University of North Carolina with a controversial reputation as an expert witness.

Stephen Buckley was first connected to the crime by Alex Hernandez in one of Alex's many and various accounts. Detective John Sam went out to see Buckley and found that the kid did in fact have a pair of boots with a similar sunburst heel pattern. But there were some subtle differences, which is why the crime lab refused to confirm the match. Meanwhile Sam tried to crack Buckley in a ferocious day-long third-degree and all he got was "I didn't do it, I didn't do it." Sam says that Stephen Buckley knows zip about the Nicarico case.

Tom Knight, however, thinks otherwise. He is convinced it was Stephen Buckley who kicked in the door at 620 Clover Court on February 25—that he and Cruz and Hernandez intended to rob the house when they discovered Jeanine Nicarico—and that they carried her off and raped her and killed her.

When he gets the report from Louise Robbins, the shoe-print expert from North Carolina, Knight finally has the solid evidence he's been waiting for. Robbins says that after making test impressions she has concluded that the three other experts who examined the boot were mistaken—the shoe worn by Stephen Buckley made the marks on the Nicarico's front door. And that does it. Robbins's testimony will place Buckley at the scene. If Knight can tie Cruz and Hernandez to the burglary, these three low-lifes will be toast.

Throughout the summer and fall of 1983, Knight presents the grand jury with a promenade of small-time outlaws as he combs East Aurora for incriminating testimony from friends and enemies of the two burglars. After six months of digging he has unearthed several reluctant witnesses who are willing to tie them to the crime. Most of these people are in trouble with the cops themselves and given Knight's power to make matters worse, they are anxious to please.[5]

A cousin will testify that Cruz told him he was there. A former cellmate will say the same thing. Alex Hernandez also has a cousin who's in trouble with the law. He says he was told that both men were there. He says Alex told him that Cruz did it.

WHEATON—MARCH 1984

It's an incredibly flimsy case based on second hand accounts. None of these witnesses is star quality, Louise Robbins included, and while there are some neighbors and highway maintenance workers whose general descriptions might work in Knight's favor, there is no confession, no eyewitness, no fingerprint that directly ties Cruz or Hernandez to the scene. But Knight has run out of time. The primary election is March 20. On a blustery Thursday less than two weeks before the election, Tom Knight asks the grand jury to indict Rolando Cruz, Alejandro Hernandez, and Stephen Buckley for the murder of Jeanine Nicarico. The panel readily complies. And over at the DuPage County crime lab, the cynics' office pool goes to the employee who picked March 8—twelve days before the election—as the moment the indictments would come down.[6]

John Sam is dismayed. It's conceivable that Knight may have something on Cruz or Hernandez that he didn't know about. But Buckley? No way. The kid is so timid he couldn't possibly have withstood Sam's brutal third-degree without cracking. Sam decides to drop by Buckley's cell.

"Steve," he says, "I know you didn't do it. And if you can think of anything I can do to prove you're innocent, let me know what it is."[7]

WHEATON—MARCH 20, 1984

Unfortunately for Tom Knight, his boss loses the primary election in spite of everyone's heroic efforts to solve the Nicarico case. In Republican DuPage County, that's the ball game. The new state's attorney will be Knight's nemesis, Jim Ryan. Everyone can hear the ax being whetted. Right after Ryan takes the oath of office he pulls Knight off the Nicarico case and installs his own man.

But Jim Ryan has completely underestimated Knight's personal political capital. Jeanine's parents, Tom and Patricia Nicarico, have come to trust Tom Knight and they don't like the idea of switching horses. Over the past year, as the Nicaricos and their neighbors mobilized to pressure various agencies and officials, they have come to understand the levers of power and how to pull them. When this group circulates a petition demanding Knight be retained, they get several thousand signatures.[8]

Jim Ryan is no dummy. He folds immediately. Tom Knight is re-appointed and given full control over the prosecution of Cruz, Hernandez and Buckley.

WHEATON—APRIL, 1984

John Sam isn't a lone voice in the wilderness. James Teal is chief of police in the village of Naperville where the crime was committed. Though he isn't directly involved in the case—his men were chased away by the sheriff on Day One—Teal knows the details and he thinks Knight has lost his bearings. In the interest of steering a friend clear of the rocks, he takes the state's attorney to lunch at the Viking Restaurant, a refuge beyond the city limits where you can legitimately buy a drink.

Chief Teal has a couple of photographs with him. After the pleasantries he lays the shots on the table. It's the shoe prints. He says, "You can tell just by looking that Buckley's shoe print is different from the print on the door."[9]

Knight shoves the photos aside without looking at them. He knows all about the different curvature of the sunburst in the heel print. His expert, Louise Robbins, has already dealt with that. She says it must have been caused by slippage of the boot as the door opened.

WHEATON—NOVEMBER, 1984

Detective John Sam has arrived at the end of his tether. For a year and a half he's been in a running battle with the prosecutor about these three defendants. Tom Knight has tried to convince him time and again that it was these three thugs who killed Jeanine Nicarico but Sam won't buy it. It was a sex crime, he says, not a robbery. He believes Jeanine's killer worked alone and, what's more, he's still out there. So Sam has been looking for him.

Which creates an embarrassing situation. Here you have the state's attorney saying it's all wrapped up, meanwhile one of his top detectives is still out chasing suspects. Sheriff Richard Doria calls Sam in and gives him an ultimatum—back Tom Knight or else. Sam says he still has serious doubts about the defendants.

"We did everything we could," says Doria. "We're shaking every tree in the forest."[10]

"Yeah," says Sam, "but I don't think we're in the right forest."

Unyielding, John Sam presses on until he's finally bumped from the case. In fact he's pulled out of homicide altogether. He's assigned to patrol convenience stores for liquor violations.

Though he loves police work and expected to spend the rest of his life at it—he still leads the department in felony arrests—he's clearly not the kind of team player this outfit is looking for. And on these terms, not likely to become one. On the first of December he hands in his badge and his gun and walks away from the job of a lifetime.[11]

WHEATON—DECEMBER 20, 1984

The State of Illinois discovered some time ago what they're just now learning down in Texas: if you plan to execute an indigent defendant it's cheaper in the long run to give him a decent lawyer. Frank Wesolowski certainly qualifies. As a public defender paid by the government to represent the defenseless, Wesolowski is as well equipped as anyone in the state to represent Alex Hernandez. He's the top man in the DuPage County public defender's office. That's the upside. The downside is, he'll still have to run the office throughout the trial.

Rolando Cruz will be represented by one of Wesolowski's deputies, Tom Laz, also a pro with nearly a decade of experience. Like his boss, Laz will have to juggle some 80 other cases, but even this seriously impaired level of attention is deemed excessive by some of the county commissioners. One day a member of the county board stops Wesolowski in the hallway and asks him why he assigned two lawyers to these low-lifes when one would be plenty.

Stephen Buckley is somewhat better off than the other two defendants. His family hires a couple of young but experienced local attorneys. Blonde, blue-eyed WASP with complimentary courtroom talents, Gary Johnson and Cliff Lund are tailor made for a law-and-order venue like this. But their outrage will overwhelm their professional caution and in the end they'll wind up working for free.

Facing them across the aging courtroom, Tom Knight and his first assistant, Patrick King, are armed to the teeth. Together they've been working on this thing for two years and there is no detail they haven't examined microscopically. With mountains of transcripts from the grand jury proceedings, they know what everybody's going to say and they have a plan for every contingency.

On the other hand, they still have a case built on toothpicks. The only physical evidence is the boot print. Everything else is conversation. Try as they might, they've never been able to get any of these creeps to admit anything. Knight has been hoping for a confession but nobody will crack. Then, just as the trial is about to begin, his prayers are answered.

At an office party five days before Christmas, Knight's assistant, Patrick King, is talking to a couple of the detectives who worked the case with John Sam. Thomas Vosburgh and Dennis Kurzawa were the two officers who picked Cruz up last year when he claimed he'd been threatened by Hernandez. As they were bringing him in, they say, Cruz made an incriminating statement about the crime. He told them he'd had a "vision" about the little girl's killing. In talking about this vision he mentioned details he could only have known if he was there. Kurzawa says that several people were told about the statement at the time but apparently everybody forgot about it.[12]

This statement, of course, is exactly what Knight needs. With two police officers on the stand to corroborate the account, it's as close to a confession as you can get without having the perp sign on the dotted line. It ties Cruz directly to the crime and anchors the whole case. A few days before the trial he files this new evidence with the court. The defense attorneys go ballistic.

This kind of last-minute blindside violates the rules of the game. Under other circumstances it would likely meet with some resistance from the court. Judge Edward Kowal, however, is in a tough spot. He's a respected jurist with a reputation for fairness but he's running for reelection himself next year. If it looks like he's more concerned about the rights of baby killers than rights of the victims, he can kiss this job goodbye.

WHEATON—JANUARY, 1985

With twelve citizens empaneled—eight women, four men—the trial opens in the old county courthouse on January 14, and the press is there in force. The case has become a sensation because it is every working mother's nightmare—a little girl dragged from her home in broad daylight. It means there's no such thing as a safe place.

In an atmosphere like this the quaint constitutional presumption of innocence pretty much goes out the window. As the three defendants walk into the packed courtroom for the first time with their attorneys, the hatred is palpable. "You could cut it with a knife," says Buckley counsel Gary Johnson.[13]

In his opening argument, State's attorney Tom Knight

proves equal to his reputation. He lays out a horrifying replay of the crime capped with a passionate and emotional appeal to reason and justice. It has a tremendous impact on everyone including Knight. And he's not faking it. After the same appeal at the end of the trial, one of Knight's colleagues will find him in the men's room weeping.

Throughout this opening volley the defense attorneys object repeatedly and are repeatedly overruled. Long before this hearing began, the defense demanded separate trials for each of their clients. The state refused, but Judge Kowal assured them that the prosecutors would not be allowed to tie the three defendants together in one sweeping statement. Knight has just done that. Nevertheless, Kowal gives the prosecutor a pass and orders the trial to proceed. But in their haste to get on with it, Kowal and Knight are sowing the seeds of their own undoing. These legalistic details are pivotal. If an objection gets into the record and it's overruled, it opens the door to an appeal.[14]

Two of Knight's key witnesses are jailbirds who spent time with Cruz, and since this sort of snitch testimony is always suspect, Knight has to show that their statements are completely voluntary. He calls the two state's attorneys who prosecuted these witnesses for the crimes that landed them in jail, and both prosecutors swear there was no quid pro quo. They assure the jury that the witnesses got no reward whatsoever for their testimony.

But memory is fallible and sometimes we only recall what we want to. The defense attorneys have located transcripts from the trials of both of these state witnesses, and the prosecutors seem to have forgotten some essential details. It turns out these witnesses went to trial shortly after they met Cruz in jail. In both cases the prosecutors pleaded for leniency for the defendants. Why? Because they were cooperating with Knight's investigation.

The closest thing Knight has to a confession is the unrecorded "vision" dialogue with Rolando Cruz when detectives Vosburgh and Kurzawa picked him up. Called to the stand, they testify that Cruz detailed several facts in his vision statement that had not been made public. Why didn't they write a report at the time? They said Knight told them not to. He told them he would bring it up before the grand jury.

Despite the explosive nature of this evidence, the prosecutor and the detectives apparently suffered a total memory wipeout the following day. Less than 12 hours after the vision conversation, Cruz was questioned extensively at the station and nobody ever brought it up. And when Knight himself grilled Cruz relentlessly in two subsequent grand jury sessions, there was not a peep about the vision statement.[15] Under other circumstances these elastic recollections might be highly suspect. But when you have three possible baby killers in the dock, everyone's inclined to give the prosecutors the benefit of the doubt.

The lynchpin of Knight's case is Louise Robbins, the boot-print expert from the University of North Carolina, and her testimony is devastating. She says that because of the way people walk, boot prints are like fingerprints—every one unique. Based on her analysis, she can confirm that the print on the Nicarico's door came from Stephen Buckley's boot.

But in a meticulous cross examination by Gary Johnson, Louise Robbins's credentials come unglued. Johnson is able to establish that her methods are based on opinion rather than science—there are no supporting studies for her theories—and her ideas have been discredited by almost every other expert in her field. Though her testimony has helped send several people up the river, her resumé suggests that she's a $1000-a-day professional witness who's made a career of supplying prosecutors with expert opinions that are hers alone.

Knight responds with a surprising countermove. Some of the same lab technicians who originally refused to confirm the match are now willing to back Louise Robbins's testimony. Eighteen months ago the man from the Kansas Bureau of Investigation refused to say the prints were identical. Now he testifies that they are.[16]

Buckley's lawyers decide to take a shot in the dark. They ask the witness for his notes. Reluctantly, the lab notes are produced and it's clear at a glance that this technician simply changed his mind for no apparent reason. His doubtfulness in the laboratory has been replaced with absolute certainty on the witness stand.

Gary Johnson opens Buckley's defense by calling his own boot-print experts. A professor of anthropology from Kent State points to dramatic differences between the two impressions. It seems there are two similar boots on the market these days, both cheap knock-offs of an expensive hiking shoe. The heel patterns are similar but the sunburst rays have a distinctly different curve. The boot that made the print on the Nicarico's door most closely matches the boot from Fayva. Stephen Buckley bought his at Payless and the heel is clearly different.

As the defense prepares to wrap it up, the atmosphere is no more reassuring than when they began. But they have been saving an ace in the hole—a single witness who can blow the prosecution's case out of the water all by himself.

Tom Knight is on his way into court when he spots a familiar face in the hall. He stops in his tracks. It's former detective John Sam—here to testify for the defense. Shaken, Knight confronts him. "What are you going to say?"

"Whatever they ask me," says Sam, "I'm going to tell them the truth."[17]

Knight turns and dashes into the courtroom. He can't allow this cop to sit on the witness stand and list his doubts about the evidence. If the jury hears that the former lead investigator thinks the snitches are unbelievable and that Cruz doesn't fit the FBI profile, the whole case will collapse. Knight is able to get an immediate order from Judge Kowal barring the former lawman from testifying about privileged information.

Checkmate. John Sam had hoped to have his day in court. One of the reasons he quit, in fact, was so he could testify for the defense. Now he can't even do that. Depressed, discouraged, he's been blocked at every turn. Now he's barred from the witness stand. "If I could have gotten up and told my story," he says, "they'd all have walked."[18]

WHEATON—FEBRUARY 22, 1985

It is two years almost to the day since Jeanine Nicarico was ripped from her home and carried away to a horrifying death. After a month of testimony and 14 hours of deliberation, the jury is back with a verdict. Cruz and Hernandez, guilty as charged. The panel is deadlocked eight-to-four on Stephen Buckley.

One of the four, an insurance broker named Michael Callahan, is appalled. He thinks Buckley is innocent and he's worried about the other two as well. He's uneasy about convicting anybody on such slender evidence but the momentum is hard to resist. "Half the jurors made up their minds on the first day of the trial," says Callahan. "There was a strong feeling that somebody had to pay for this."[19]

Callahan, however, is not interested in becoming

famous as the lone holdout, so he goes along with the others on Cruz and Hernandez. But he still has plenty of reservations and he has a plan to limit the damage. During the sentencing phase of the trial, he is resolved to stand fast. He will deny the prosecutors the unanimous vote they must have for the death penalty. He wants to keep these two guys alive just in case.

Unfortunately the defense attorneys know nothing of Callahan's doubts and they make an understandable but disastrous error. Because of the inflamed state of public opinion, they decide they can't trust the jury. They agree to let Judge Kowal decide on the penalty. The jury is dismissed.

The Nicarico family has been pulverized by this tragedy, and they get their chance to take the witness stand during the penalty phase. Their agony saturates the courtroom. Their pain, and the accounts of other witnesses about statements that Cruz and Hernandez apparently made to their jailers before, during, and after the trial, paints such a monstrous picture of the defendants that the judge has little choice. After deliberating 10 minutes, he brings down the hammer: death by lethal injection.[20]

Throughout the trial, Rolando Cruz has had a street punk arrogance about him that did not serve him well with the jury. Now that's all gone. Sobbing, both he and Hernandez have to be helped to their feet.

WHEATON—JUNE, 1985

With Cruz and Hernandez safely entombed downstate in Menard Prison and Buckley locked up awaiting retrial, parents in the western suburbs are just beginning to breath a little easier. But on June 2, less than three months after the conviction, their illusions are shattered. Seven-year-old Melissa Ackerman is snatched off her bike in broad daylight near a small town west of Aurora. Two weeks later they find her body in a drainage ditch. She was sexually assaulted and drowned.

John Sam always thought the killer was still out there. He may not be a cop anymore but his mind is still on the job. When he hears that a 28-year-old ex-con named Brian Dugan is about to be charged with Melissa Ackerman's rape and murder, he calls his old boss at the sheriff's station. Sam says if he was still on the case he'd have somebody check this guy out.

Detective Warren Wilkosz, lead investigator on the Nicarico case, takes the assignment. The next morning he stops by the LaSalle County Jail to meet this fellow Dugan. Wilkosz says he's here about the Nicarico murder. He wants to know if Dugan has an alibi for February 25, 1983. Dugan immediately clams up. He wants to talk to his lawyer.

Wilkosz's next move is to ring up the Illinois Department of Corrections. He learns that Dugan got out of prison six months before the Nicarico murder. On parole, Dugan had been working a factory job, so Wilkosz runs by the plant to check out his time cards. He finds that on the day Jeanine Nicarico disappeared, Dugan didn't come to work. Wilkosz checks the motor-vehicle records. In 1983, Dugan was driving a green Plymouth Volare, a match for the description given by highway workers who spotted a suspicious car near the hiking trail.[21]

A reaction like that would normally pique a cop's curiosity, but Warren Wilkosz apparently decides he already knows too much about Brian Dugan's involvement in the Nicarico case. He heads back to the office and shuts down his investigation without bothering to write a report.[22]

Objective reality, however, has a way of intruding on our most carefully constructed fantasies, and the Brian

Dugan case is about to blow the lid off the criminal justice system in DuPage County. In the course of plea-bargaining over the murder of Melissa Ackerman, Dugan is beginning to talk and he is spinning a horrifying tale of serial rape and murder. To avoid the death penalty, he's already pleading guilty to raping and killing Melissa Ackerman and another woman. Then, on November 15, he drops the bomb. His lawyer says Dugan is willing to plead guilty in the Nicarico case. He killed her, he says. He acted alone. Those three other guys had nothing to do with it.[23]

WHEATON—NOVEMBER, 1985

Imagine now the gut-wrenching fear oozing through the DuPage County prosecutor's office. If they accept Dugan at his word, it means that Knight and his people somehow managed to frame two innocent men. It means the "vision" statement is a hoax. It means cops were lying on the witness stand. It means that all that testimony from those small time hoods was coerced. It means the Black Knight has led the Nicarico family down a dreadful dead end trail. Since this option is unacceptable, there has to be some other explanation.

The most dangerous threat to the prosecution's version of events is Illinois State Police Lieutenant Ed Cisowski, the man assigned to look into Dugan's confession. Cisowski, a fifteen-year veteran, is the department's chief investigator for northeastern Illinois, and at first he is as skeptical as Tom Knight. But as he begins digging he realizes that there are too many details that Dugan is able to hit right on the button. True, he's got a few things wrong. He doesn't recall the boat in the driveway, and he got the staircase reversed. But he knows it was a piece of rotten cloth that was used for the blindfold and he can describe exactly how it was fastened with serrated medical tape. He knows about the upstairs bedroom where Jeanine was tied up and about the tan sheet that was ripped off the bed to hide her. And he's able to tell them that "Sleepy" was the Dwarf on her nightie. When a couple of Cisowski's troopers load Dugan in a patrol car and ask him to find the victim's house, he directs them unerringly to the Nicarico residence on Clover Court, then on to the hiking trail where the girl was bludgeoned to death. Dugan says he killed her with a tire iron.

Cisowski, convinced now that Dugan is the lone killer, lays the case before the DuPage County authorities. They cut him off at the knees. Sheriff Richard Doria simply gets up and walks out of the room. State's Attorney Jim Ryan and assistant Robert Kilander are a little more courteous, but barely. Kilander says he's already met with Dugan's attorney and Dugan is a liar.[24]

Cisowski is dumbfounded. But then he's just a simple cop like John Sam. Had he been more politically astute he might have noticed the ax swinging for his neck.

WHEATON—DECEMBER, 1985

Tom Knight, the man at the center of this vortex, is no longer on the scene and neither is his boss, Mike Fitzsimmons. They've both moved on to other careers. So Jim Ryan could conceivably blame all this on the previous regime and let the chips fall where they may, but not without a certain political cost. It would leave Sheriff Doria and his men in the lurch—exposed as perjurers and witness tamperers—and that would cost Ryan dearly among his law and order constituents.

With the *Chicago Tribune* and the *Sun-Times* all over the place, it's time for Ryan to circle the wagons. The first line of defense calls for an assault on Lt. Cisowski's credibility. Robert Kilander, the assistant state's attorney who has taken over from Tom Knight, opens with a blast at Cisowski's investigation and implies that somebody must be feeding Dugan details about the crime and that somebody might be Lt. Cisowski. The attack gets a boost when it's joined by Jeanine's parents. From the beginning, Thomas and Patricia Nicarico have kept faith with the prosecutors and they have certainly held up their end of the log. They were there for every pretrial hearing and every excruciating day of the trial and sentencing. The idea that this could all be some stupid mistake is simply not acceptable.

When Lt. Cisowski began his investigation, the Nicaricos were supportive because they thought that Brian Dugan might somehow have been involved. But when they realize that Cisowski and Dugan are saying Dugan did it alone, they distance themselves immediately. The whole idea is unbearable. It would mean that the three men they've come to despise more than anything on earth would just walk out of jail scott free. A plea bargain with Dugan would obviously rule out the death penalty. And since he's already got life, it would be, in a weird way, almost as if nobody would be paying for Jeanine's death at all. Says Cisowski, "Once the Nicarico's found out there was no death row, everything changed."[25]

WHEATON—AUGUST, 1986

The case against Stephen Buckley, still in the lockup after his hung jury eighteen months earlier, is further undermined when the FBI crime lab comes down on the side of the defense. The agency's top expert says the boot prints don't match. If the Brian Dugan confession gets to the jury during Buckley's retrial, it could be a knockout blow for the defense, and Robert Kilander is determined to suppress it.

At the preliminary hearing for the retrial, Kilander tears

into Lt. Cisowski's testimony and highlights the inconsisten-cies. He says there was a 22-foot sailboat in the driveway and Dugan didn't remember it. The little girl's nightie was white, not pink. She wasn't wearing toenail polish, it was fingernail polish. Cisowski counters with a laundry list of details Dugan has provided that could only be known to the killer.

DuPage County Circuit Judge Robert A. Nolan will preside over the Buckley retrial and he's a long-time friend and colleague of former prosecutor Mike Fitzsimmons. Nolan doesn't like what the press is saying about Fitzsimmons, or about this case and the DuPage County courts in general, so he issues a gag order forbidding anybody from talking about it. After hearing all the evidence he decides Dugan was lying—"a bad actor on a stage," he says. He dismisses Dugan's confession as a sick attempt to attract attention. It will not be permitted at Buckley's trial.

By mid-September jury selection is underway in Judge Nolan's courtroom when the prosecutors drop another grenade. It seems they have two new jailhouse snitches who overheard Stephen Buckley confess to the crime. Outraged, the defense demands time to respond and the trial is aborted.

Before it can resume, the prosecution takes another unexpected hit on the waterline. Professor Melvin Lewis of John Marshall Law School, a national authority on forensic science, has called together a panel of criminologists and anthropologists to specifically examine the courtroom testi-mony of shoe-print expert Louise Robbins. The panel con-cludes that her assumptions "cannot be sustained" and her methods are unsound. Professor Lewis himself is more direct: "It seems the only standard the courts are requiring of foren-sic science is that it be incriminating to the defendant."[26]

Buckley's defense team, meanwhile, has been unearthing all kinds of interesting items that the prosecutors have forgotten to tell them about, including the notes of several crime lab experts who argued against Knight's theories from the beginning. In the spring of 1987 the defense files a motion to dismiss based on prosecutorial misconduct. On March 5, as the team heads for court to argue the motion, the prosecutors tell them to forget about it. DuPage County has had enough of Stephen Buckley. All charges are withdrawn. After three years in prison he's free to go.

The Nicaricos, understandably, are outraged. They publicly blast the state's attorney for this debacle. Heading for the tall grass, Jim Ryan calls a press conference and blames it all on legal technicalities, defense treachery, and the fact that star witness Louise Robbins has cancer and could not testify. Ryan takes pains to point out that Buckley's dismissal had nothing to do with Brian Dugan or his confession. Dugan is lying, that's been established by Judge Nolan, and his evil deception will have no effect whatsoever on the status of Cruz or Hernandez.[27]

SPRINGFIELD, ILLINOIS—JANUARY, 1988

Every death penalty verdict in Illinois runs through an automatic appeal process, and four years after the verdict the state Supreme Court has come to the conclusion that Rolando Cruz and Alex Hernandez did not get a fair hearing. As the defense lawyers argued from the outset, Cruz and Hernandez were entitled to separate trials because they made incriminating statements about each other. The defense attorneys couldn't cross examine either one because they were being tried together. The high court rules for the defense and orders a new trial. Everybody is sent back to square one.[28]

WHEATON—SUMMER, 1989

The retrial of Rolando Cruz is again in the hands of Judge Edward Kowal. The defense team, growing by leaps and bounds as the case gathers national attention, is now headed by Michael Metnick and Jed Stone, a powerful and flamboyant courtroom heavyweight in every sense of the term. His first face-off with Robert Kilander is over the Brian Dugan confession. Once again Kilander goes after the inconsistencies and hammers the point that Dugan is a lying sicko, but the corroborating evidence is piling up. A plaster cast of the tire treads from the hiking trail is the same as the tires that would have been on Dugan's Plymouth, and a couple of significant forensic scientists have concluded that the murder weapon could have been a tire iron, just as Dugan said.

With the Chicago press corps now in full cry, Judge Kowal is not in a position to be as casually dismissive of Dugan's claim as Judge Nolan was. He agrees to let the jury hear the confession.

In the midst of preparing for the contest, Cruz's defense team gets a tip that the prosecutor might still be withholding some useful information. Attorney Jed Stone confronts Kilander. After threatening to file a motion in court, he shakes loose a sheaf of notes from a meeting that took place between Kilander and Brian Dugan's attorney back in November of 1985. The notes reveal that Dugan, at that very first meeting, laid the story out for the prosecutor in elaborate detail, itemizing 51 specific facts about the Nicarico kidnap and murder. And that meeting took place on the 13th—two days before Lt. Cisowski ever met Dugan—so the idea that Cisowski had somehow fed information to Dugan was obviously false and Kilander knew it.

ROCKFORD, ILLINOIS—JANUARY, 1990

The Cruz trial has been moved an hour northwest to Winnebago County in the hope of finding an unbiased jury but the new venue is unable to shed the old political baggage. From the outset Judge Kowal rules repeatedly for Kilander. To lawyer Jed Stone it seems clear that the judge and prosecutor are in lockstep on this thing. For some reason they seem determined to get a conviction, even at the risk of another reversal.

In the face of the accumulating evidence, it's becoming more and more difficult for the prosecution to sell the idea that Brian Dugan made all this up. It's time to move on to option two. In his opening argument, Robert Kilander pulls a stunning reversal. He says that if the evidence shows that Brian Dugan is not lying about the murder of Jeanine Nicarico, all that means is that he was there—*along with Rolando Cruz and Alex Hernandez.*

The defense is dumbfounded. Prepared to argue that Dugan did it alone, they are caught flat-footed by this line of attack. But to support this theory, a lot of the testimony from the first trial will have to be altered to fit the new facts. At the first trial Kilander maintained that the victim died at the hiking trail. Now he says she was killed somewhere else and dumped there. Judge Kowal accepts this sudden flip without comment. What's more, he refuses to let the defense even mention it to the jury.

The Cruz "vision" statement is re-introduced and embellished. The two detectives now remember that right after they heard the statement, they called their boss, Sgt. James Montesano, and told him about it.

Though Judge Kowal agreed to let the Dugan confession be heard, the testimony from State Police investigator Ed Cisowski is interrupted by so many objections that the jury gets only fragments. Dugan's guilt is no longer out of bounds but anything suggesting that he acted alone is disallowed. The well-established fact that this kind of crime is almost invariably committed by a loner is completely suppressed. No FBI profilers or sex crime experts are permitted to testify.

The most important witness in this contest isn't here. Brian Dugan offered to take the stand and tell all but only if DuPage County promises not to kill him. So Kilander is able to keep him away from the jury by simply refusing to grant him immunity. Without immunity Dugan understandably takes the Fifth.

With the defense off balance, Kilander delivers the decisive blow. He's found a prisoner who says he heard a jailyard confession that will tie the three men together. Death row inmate Robert Turner says Cruz spilled the whole story to him while they were in the exercise yard three years ago.

Turner's narrative is so revolting it paints Cruz as a perverted monster who enjoyed every minute of the rape and murder. Turner insists his testimony is purely voluntary, that he's getting no reward, but once again the prosecutors are biting their tongues. Turner, desperate to get off death row, has a promise from Kilander that he will speak up for Turner at his next hearing.[29] Since this information would significantly weaken Turner's credibility, the state's attorney keeps it to himself.

The case goes to the jury at the end of the third week and for the twelve citizens of Winnebago County it's a fairly easy call. The testimony of the police officers is more or less taken at face value. Why would they lie?

For the second time Rolando Cruz is convicted of the murder of Jeanine Nicarico and sentenced to death. Jed Stone is shaken to his boots. He's an experienced and talented defense attorney but Kilander has danced rings around him. At one point the state introduced some photos of footprints found near the side window of the Nicarico house, but Kilander waited until the very last moment of his rebuttal to suggest that these footprints belonged to Cruz—too late for Stone to counter or object.

Had Jed Stone taken a step back for a view of the big picture he might have realized what was going on here, but for a Chicago boy he seems remarkably naive about the stakes on the table. Kilander's boss, Jim Ryan, intends to be the next Illinois Attorney General. That leaves zero tolerance for courtroom fuckups in the county's most notorious case. When the jury foreman says "guilty," Robert Kilander slams his fist on the table in triumph.

BLOOMINGTON, ILLINOIS—APRIL, 1990

The retrial of Alex Hernandez has been moved downstate to McLean County but Robert Kilander is still the point man and Judge Kowal is still on the bench. With the stakes rising at each turn of the cards, Kilander is able once again to come up with several last-minute witnesses who overheard Hernandez confess to the crime. One is a jailhouse snitch—apparently never in short supply for the DuPage prosecutors—but the others are sheriff's detectives who worked the case with John Sam. These men failed to show up at the first trial and they didn't bother to write contemporaneous reports about what they heard, but their recollections now are specific, detailed, and damning.

There are also the usual stunning revelations of prosecutorial sleight-of-hand. The shoe prints outside the window that Kilander had made so much of in the final moments of the Cruz trial turn out to be *women's* shoe prints. Kilander used photos of these prints to suggest that Cruz peeked in the side window before the break in, but these Nike prints were female size six—an impossible fit for Cruz or Hernandez.

The jury in Bloomington is not as pliant as the one in Rockford and they can't reach a verdict. Kowal declares a mistrial. Hernandez is still in limbo but the state's case is starting to unravel.

ROCK ISLAND, ILLINOIS—APRIL, 1991

The third Hernandez trial is moved across the state to the Mississippi River town of Rock Island and this time the defense manages to get a brand new judge. John J. Nelligan is a bit more even-handed than his predecessor and the prosecutors actually lose some of the pretrial arguments. Once again the DuPage County detectives take the stand to repeat and embellish the various confessions they have overheard, but this time the defense is able to seriously damage the state's key witness. Using transcripts from the previous trials, they show how Sheriff's Lieutenant Robert Winkler has told two completely different stories.

With the prosecutors rattled, the Hernandez team thinks it smells victory. So after a lengthy debate they decide to rest the case without putting on a defense. This dramatic gesture, they are convinced, will show the jury that the state's case is so weak it's not worthy of a response. It is a catastrophic blunder. Once again the jurors have little choice but to believe the cops and this time they all agree. The verdict is "guilty." And there is plenty of guilt to go around. The defense team is mortified that they blew the opportunity to tell the jury about Brian Dugan.

Judge Nelligan decides to head for the middle of the road. He's bothered by the fact that there's not a shred of physical evidence tying Hernandez to the scene and the fact that the whole case is built on a skein of disconnected ramblings from a notorious liar with an I.Q. of 65. Nelligan won't go for death. He gives Hernandez 80 years.

CHICAGO—DECEMBER, 1991

In its entire history the Illinois Supreme Court has never granted anyone a third trial in a death penalty case, so a reversal in the Rolando Cruz conviction will require the services of a legal wizard. Fortunately for Cruz there happens to be one ready at hand. The case has become the talk of La Salle Street and major downtown law firms like Jenner and Block are being solicited for assistance. But the White Knight who now appears on the chessboard turns out to be a law school professor from Northwestern University. Larry Marshall, a bearded 31-year-old Jewish intellectual, is considered an authority on judicial ethics despite his youth. He served as law clerk to U.S. Supreme Court Justice John Paul Stevens.

Digging through the history of the case, Marshall is dismayed. It seems obvious on its face: Cruz is innocent, Dugan is guilty. What's more, the record is so riddled with errors he can't see how the high court will be able to turn down a third trial, precedent or not.

Riding herd on a mushrooming army of lawyers, investigators and student volunteers, Marshall organizes a microscopic dissection of the trial transcripts. Robert Kilander's skill at bait-and-switch becomes apparent, but more significantly, they can see how Judge Kowal's rulings effectively gutted Dugan's confession. The jury was not allowed to hear that Dugan had kidnapped other young girls like Jeanine Nicarico, or that his M.O. included kicking in doors, or that he blindfolded and wrapped his victims in blankets, or that he raped and sodomized and killed them—and that he always worked alone.

As the filing deadline approaches in the fall of 1991, Marshall's appellate team is pulling 80-hour weeks to refine the massive brief and in the closing days they hardly bother to leave the office at all. One of the lead attorneys personally drives the bound copies to the Supreme Court in Springfield, then they settle in to wait for the state's response. And as they wait, the case explodes again onto the front pages.

CHICAGO—MARCH, 1992

Mary Brigid Kenney is the bright new lawyer in the Illinois Attorney General's office who's been tapped to write the state's response to the Cruz brief. She's been at it now for some time, digging through the same 10,000-page transcript the professor went through, and try as she might she can't seem to swallow the prosecution's argument. Instead, she has come to the same conclusion as Larry Marshall. There's no case here. No physical evidence. No blood, no fingerprints, no nada. Only innuendo, hearsay, witness manipulation... and maybe worse. Then one day, skimming through the most recent trail, it hits her like a sledgehammer. All the evidence clearly points to Brian Dugan. He killed this little girl and he killed her alone. And not a shred of this evidence was presented to the jury that convicted Rolando Cruz and sentenced him to death.

Stunned, she gets up from her desk. "We have a Bill of Rights!" she says. "This is the United States of America!" She heads for the office of Terry Madsen, the chief of criminal appeals, and breaks the bad news. He's unimpressed. He advises her to think it over. He tells her to go ahead and write the brief, and if she still feels the same way when she's done, she won't have to argue it in court. He'll find somebody else.

Dazed, Kenney talks to one of her colleagues. He agrees with Madsen. "Sometimes," he says, "you just have to take a case and argue it and hope desperately that you lose it."[30]

This is a new experience for Kenney. The topic at hand is the lethal injection of a man who is probably innocent of the crime and the only thing these people are able to focus on is their professional responsibility to support the prosecutor.

She fires off a memo to the head man, Illinois Attorney General Roland Burris. She says the safest course for everyone involved would be to drop this thing like a hot potato. The state should confess error and let Cruz walk.

Burris won't hear of it. He insists on a full court press.

Her colleagues advise her to go with the flow but Mary Brigid Kenney wasn't raised that way. And that's always a source of heartburn for career politicians like Burris—the occasional oddball who slips in under the radar, the independent thinker who will not retool his or her moral compass to fit the program. It's the X-factor that somehow makes the country work in spite of itself.

Since Kenney will be giving up a job she loves, she decides to go out with a bang. Her letter of resignation is so simple and straightforward that it winds up on the front page of the *Chicago Sun-Times*.

"I cannot sit idly as this office continues to pursue the unjust prosecution and execution of Rolando Cruz," she writes. The trials "were infected by many instances of prosecutorial misconduct."[31]

Overall, the press coverage is starting to get vicious. The Cruz case has become a tar-baby that sticks to everybody who touches it. Burris would probably like to duck but he can't. He's planning a run for governor. How would it look if he became famous for springing a baby killer? It's not hard to imagine his opponent's ad campaign. Burris calls a press conference and tries to dismiss Kenney's accusations by questioning her motives and her competence.

SPRINGFIELD, ILLINOIS—JUNE, 1992

Larry Marshall and his team have been rehearsing the oral arguments before moot courts and fellow experts for weeks and they are ready for anything. But when they finally go before the Supreme Court and Marshall delivers his emotional appeal for a retrial, the seven jurists sit in stony silence. They don't ask a single question.

The state responds by demanding an execution date. Then the enigmatic judges retire from the scene to deliberate and the lawyers head back to Chicago. Everybody on Marshall's team says his presentation was masterful but there is unspoken nervousness about the lack of response from the court.

Six months later they're summoned back to the Supreme Court. On the morning of December 4 as they wait for the building to open they're surrounded on the steps by camera crews and reporters and crackling suspense. The doors open, Marshall dashes through the crush, grabs a copy of the opinion, flips to the bottom line—and he's thunderstruck. A 4-to-3 majority has voted to let the conviction stand. No new trial for Cruz. The death penalty is affirmed.

The opinion was written by Justice James D. Heiple, an arch-conservative among the conservative majority on the court, and it is basically a restatement of the prosecution's argument—Brian Dugan's confession is irrelevant. Cruz has been convicted by two juries, end of story. But in the course of building support for his position, Justice Heiple begins to fantasize. He cites the "overwhelming physical evidence" connecting Cruz directly to the crime—an astounding statement since lack of physical evidence has been a salient flaw in the case from the outset. Heiple's opinion implies either ignorance of the facts or ignorance of the law and it is so over the top it backfires.

Lawyers, scholars and commentators from all over the state are inflamed by this distortion. Larry Marshall, still recovering from the decision, soon finds himself in command of a powerful legal engine. His petition for rehearing is now joined by the majority of the state's law school deans, fifteen former prosecutors, and the leaders of two dozen major religious groups including Cardinal Joseph Bernardine of the Archdiocese of Chicago. The television coverage and the triphammer columns from Thomas Frisbie of the *Sun-Times* and Eric Zorn of the *Tribune* have turned the Rolando Cruz saga into a *cause celebre*. Now the West Coast is calling. Actors John Cusack, Tim Robbins and Susan Sarandon are joining the chorus.

The 27-page petition for rehearing, polished to a diamond finish, is filed in Springfield on February 4, 1993. It concludes not with a plea for Cruz but with a plea for the court to save itself—to restore public confidence in the legal system.

Over the next three interminable months, Larry Marshall slips slowly into a deep depression. This is the end of the road. If he fails here, there's almost no chance the federal judiciary will intervene. His client, a man he firmly believes is innocent, will die at the hands of the state. Deep in the valley of the shadow of death, Marshall begins seeing a psychiatrist.

Then the phone rings. It's a message from Springfield. The Illinois Supreme Court has granted a rehearing. Like Grant at Appomattox, Marshall suddenly finds his crushing headache has vanished.

SPRINGFIELD—JUNE, 1993

The court has changed composition since the last round but Justice Heiple is still on the bench and he's not happy.

Throughout Marshall's oral argument, Heiple refuses to look at him. He fixes his eye on the ceiling. His sense of decorum apparently prevents him from putting his fingers in his ears. What he hears, like it or not, is a litany of repudiation. When one of the other justices asks the attorney general if there is any physical evidence connecting Rolando Cruz to the crime, the state must admit that no such evidence exists.[32]

It takes a full year for the court to get around to a decision but on July 14—Bastille Day, 1994—the new majority pulls the rug out from under Justice Heiple. In a 4-3 split in favor of Rolando Cruz, they order another trial.

CHICAGO—AUGUST, 1994

Prepping for trial number three, Larry Marshall has the cream of the crop at his disposal. Even though everybody's working for free, top flight attorneys are lined up to volunteer. Some of them see this as a defining moment for their profession. If the state is allowed to execute someone with the facts this shrouded in doubt, it speaks of some fundamental rot in the timbers. The defense team, led by former Republican prosecutor Tom Breen, quickly takes on the sheen of a corporate hit squad. Once again every word in the record is parsed and this time a vast indexing system makes it possible to quickly cross-check what everybody said about everything. Dossiers are prepared on each player containing their every pronouncement over the last decade along with copies of all reports where their name comes up.

The other side, however, has not been idle. They have a new witness. In what has come to be a widely-anticipated miracle almost as dependable as Christmas, the DuPage County prosecutors have located another snitch. This one will swear that Cruz told him he and Hernandez and Dugan were all in it together. But the detectives are apparently scraping the bottom of the barrel. As soon as this ex-con is approached by the defense team's investigators, he folds. He says one of the detectives threatened to send him back to jail if he didn't follow the script.

Adding to the prosecution's anxiety, some of the other key witnesses are coming unstuck. Steven Pecararo was in jail with Cruz back in 1983 and he testified in both trials that Cruz confessed. But there are rumors that he's having second thoughts. The defense investigators take a run out to Pecararo's suburban pawn shop and when they confront him he breaks down in tears. He begs them to apologize to Rolando. He says the prosecutors told him what to say.

At this point DuPage County Sheriff's Detective Warren Wilkosz gets word of this development and he's not happy. Wilkosz has about as much invested in this case as anyone. He was there at the beginning. He and John Sam were hanging out in the sheriff's office on that awful day 12 years ago when word came in that Jeanine was missing. It was due to the diligent efforts of Wilkosz, lead detective in the case, that many of these prosecution witnesses were unearthed. So when he hears that one of his major informants has decided to recant, he's got to find out what's up. He stops by Pecararo's pawn shop and demands some answers. Why did Pecararo flip? Did the defense attorneys threaten to nail him for perjury? Because if that's the case, says Wilkosz, his side "can play hardball too, and says, 'Well fuck you, we'll arrest you for perjury.'"

Despite the naked threat, Pecararo doesn't flinch. He knows something that Wilkosz doesn't. The pawn shop surveillance camera over his shoulder is picking up every word. When the transcript of this little chat shows up on the front page of the *Chicago Tribune* eight weeks later, the headline reads, "Tape Sinks DuPage Cop Deeper into the Ooze of Lies."[33]

Disintegrating credibility is not the only problem for Wilkosz. The new judge on the case is not one the prosecutors would have picked either. Edward Kowal, the previous overseer, has been promoted so he's above it all. Judge Nelligan refuses to get near it. Several of his colleagues head for the weeds along with him and the case bounces down the steps to Judge Ronald Mehling. To some spectators the youthful Mehling looks a lot like actor Harry Anderson, the 30-something judge on "Night Court."

History teaches us that decent human beings can show up almost anywhere but in the political playground of the DuPage County courthouse, Judge Mehling is a rare find indeed. His pretrial rulings, transparent, reasonable, even-handed, are a disaster for the prosecution. Among other things, the Brian Dugan confession will be heard in its entirety.

The impact of Dugan's statement is far more ominous for the prosecution now than when it first came up nine years ago because of the new science of genetic matching. Using DNA samples from all the suspects and comparing them with sperm swabs from the body of Jeanine Nicarico, the nation's top expert says that the man who raped her was not Rolando Cruz. It was almost certainly Brian Dugan.

The prosecutors, however, have yet another ace in the hole. Over defense objections, Cruz's "vision" statement is also allowed in evidence and this time it will be strengthened by the addition of a new corroborating witness. Detective Wilkosz's boss, Sgt. James Montesano, has not testified about this before but now he's going to back up the two detectives who heard Cruz confess. Montesano will confirm that he learned about this vision from Vosburgh and Kurzawa when they phoned him on that Friday night, May 9, back in 1983, right after Cruz made the statement.

There is, however, one curious glitch in the story. That date can't be right. Randy Garrett, a defense investigator who has followed the case from the beginning, notes that May 9, 1983 was not a Friday. It was a Monday. Was this a simple mistake on Montesano's part or is something going on here?

CHICAGO—OCTOBER, 1994

Alex Hernandez, meanwhile, has been taken off death row but he's still locked up in Galesburg on an 80-year sentence. His defense team is looking for a high-profile lawyer to mount another appeal and they hit the jackpot with Scott Turow. A former federal prosecutor and best-selling author—*Presumed Innocent, Burden of Proof*—Turow is one of the most famous attorneys in the country. At first he resists getting involved but after he reads the transcript he's a man on fire.

"I had never seen anything like it," says Turow. "When I got to Robert Kilander and those shoe prints and the business of putting a witness on the stand to testify that they were size 6 shoes—and never informing the defense that it was a *women's* size 6—I thought that stuff had gone out in the early nineteen thirties."[34]

Since Hernandez is no longer facing death, his petition goes to the appellate court, in this case a three-judge panel in suburban Elgin west of O'Hare International Airport. As with the Cruz defense, Turow is able to attract an impressive array of volunteer legal horsepower. He has over a dozen lawyers just studying the law and another gang compiling a catalogue of prosecutorial malfeasance.

Oral arguments are set for January 4, 1995 in Elgin. In the audience to watch the fireworks are several members of the Cruz team including Larry Marshall. They're about to get their money's worth. Turow, making sure nobody can accuse him of trading on celebrity, demonstrates an impressive mastery of the case and his documentation of prosecutorial double-dealing and judicial error is an indictment of everything about this mess from day one.

The prosecution responds with an argument based largely on technicalities—Dugan's confession can't be used now, they say, because the defense didn't introduce it at Hernandez's last trial—but the court isn't buying it. In one of those rare scenes where righteousness erupts just like in the movies, the judges mop the floor with the state's attorney. Two weeks later the court issues an order overturning the conviction of Alex Hernandez. He will get a fourth trial.

WHEATON—OCTOBER, 1995

Like a gut-shot rhino propelled by its own momentum, the state's case staggers onward simply because nothing seems to be able to stop it. By now so many political careers are on the line that Jeanine Nicarico and Rolando Cruz and Alex Hernandez have become mere bit players in the drama. "Whatever the verdict," says the *Chicago Tribune*, "the political repercussions could reach to one of the state's highest elected offices."[35] Jim Ryan, elected as DuPage County state's attorney just as the Cruz case was getting underway, used his record there as a springboard for the Attorney General's office. Now they say he's gearing up to run for governor or possibly the U.S. Senate. If the press turns this into open season on prosecutors, Ryan may be the biggest duck sitting on the fence but he's certainly not alone.

The third trial of Rolando Cruz, meanwhile, gets underway in Judge Mehling's courtroom on Tuesday, October 24. Larry Marshall has assembled a team of judicial all-stars including Tom Breen, Nan Nolan, and Matt Kennelly, a prominent Chicago lawyer who was first in his class at Harvard. Kennelly, like Marshall and Turow, was inflamed by the transcript. He is convinced that the state's whole case is a lie and he is preparing to take the prosecution apart witness by witness. He has plenty of ammo.

There will be no jury. The defense team was so impressed with Mehling's pretrial rulings they call for a bench trial. Let the judge decide. Cruz hasn't had much luck with juries.

In court to watch opening arguments is Ruben "Hurricane" Carter, recently freed from a murder conviction himself in a famous struggle against an out-of-control prosecution. The former middleweight championship contender has been counseling Cruz in prison.

Across the aisle, at the rail behind the prosecutor's table, are the victim's parents, Tom and Patricia Nicarico, still waiting for justice after all these years. Through each grisly hearing they have been rock solid in their determination to honor Jeanine's memory and to see that the killers pay the ultimate price. This will be the sixth trial they have endured, the sixth time they have had to sit through the excruciating reconstruction of their daughter's final hour, the sixth time they have had to face those horrible photographs. The suffering, the anger, the frustration hangs in the courtroom like an acrid cloud.

Facing the Cruz team is First Assistant State's Attorney John Kinsella. Mr. Kinsella and his colleagues have a formidable task. In the light of DNA evidence pointing to Brian Dugan, his best argument is that Dugan had help and that Cruz must have been there because so many people said so. His theory, threaded through a rambling two-hour opening argument, seems to be that a gang of burglars, Cruz among them, kicked in the door, found the girl, and didn't steal anything. They took the girl instead and turned her over to Brian Dugan who raped her. Then she was killed, and somebody, possibly Cruz, took her body and dumped it near the hiking trail.[36]

It is a concept, as Kennelly points out, unique in the annals of crime. "It defies logic," he says. "It lacks common sense."[37]

Over the next week and a half the defense team shreds the prosecution's case with surgical cross-examination. Breen and Kennelly's intimate familiarity with the testimony from the previous trials is devastating. When the medical examiner testifies that Jeanine was killed somewhere else and her body dumped along the hiking trail, Kennelly reads him a quote from the first trial where he swore the exact opposite was true. One after another, the state's experts are tripped by their own words, undone by transcripts that show they've tailored their testimony to fit the occasion.

The prosecution, however, still holds a deadly weapon in reserve—the Cruz "vision" statement. In each of the previous trials, the testimony of detectives Vosburgh and Kurzawa proved fatal, and now Lieutenant Montesano will be a powerful new corroborating witness. Matt Kennelly, in a blistering confrontation, manages to dent Vosburgh's credibility but the detective won't crack. He insists that Cruz told him details about the crime that only the killer could have known.

With this setup Lieutenant Montesano's testimony could be devastating. He has a reputation for honesty and if he says that Vosburgh and Kurzawa called him at home after they talked to Cruz on May 9, 1983, it could lock down the "vision" statement. The tension is heightened when Montesano's appearance is repeatedly delayed. Finally, Judge Mehling forces the prosecutors to produce the witness. When Montesano shows up at the end of the week, drawn and haggard, it looks like he hasn't slept in days.

Rumors of a major break have rocked the courthouse all morning and the place is packed. As press and spectators listen in slack-jawed amazement, Sergeant Montesano testifies that he made a mistake. He says he got to thinking about it last week and he checked some old credit card receipts and discovered that he could not have received the phone call at home from Detectives Vosburgh and Kurzawa on Monday, May 9, 1983, as he testified earlier. He was not *at* home. He was in Orlando, Florida.

Suddenly it is crystal clear why the prosecution tried to pretend that May 9 was a Friday. Detective Montesano was already on record saying he left for vacation Friday evening.

It's one of those stop-the-presses moments right out of Ben Hecht's *Front Page*, but this time it's for real. The defense immediately moves for a directed verdict of acquittal. The judge calls for a recess.

Thirty minutes later he reenters the courtroom and it's standing room only. Judge Mehling asks the bailiff to hand him "people's Exhibit One." It's a photograph. He holds it up for everyone to see—a picture of Jeanine Nicarico, smiling, lively, taken a few days before she died. It is a gripping reminder of what this case was supposed to be about and in Mehling's hand it is a stark rebuke to the state.

Labeling the government's case a tapestry of lies, he asks, "Is there any physical evidence in connection with this case, anything at all that connects this hideous crime and connects Mr. Cruz? Anything? Fingerprints, blood spots, blood, DNA, hair, fibers, clothes, something left there, something taken from the home that he had? Anything? Anything at all...? There is none. There is absolutely none."

Calling the day's revelations "unique in the annals of criminal justice," Mehling is barely able to contain his rage. "Did Cruz ever make the dream statement? I don't think I need to answer that because I'm going to enter a finding of not guilty and he will be discharged today. Case is closed."

WHEATON—DECEMBER 8, 1995

Confronted with the collapse of the case against Rolando Cruz, DuPage County Judge Thomas Callum dismisses all charges against Alejandro Hernandez. After twelve years in prison he is a free man.

CHICAGO—DECEMBER, 1996

The press gives professor Larry Marshall a great deal of the credit for saving Rolando Cruz but Marshall gives a great deal of credit to the press. "The coverage in the *Tribune* and the *Sun-Times*," he says, "created the atmosphere and the political space that allowed the Illinois Supreme Court to finally do what should be done."[38]

As a result of the professor's ten year back-alley tour of the criminal justice system, he will go on to become one of the major figures in the campaign to end the death penalty. But few others who stood up for Cruz and Hernandez will escape the wrath of the Establishment. Detective John Sam—ultimately proven right about everything—finds that nobody will hire him to do the work he loves. He settles for a job as a heating company sales manager. Mary Brigid Kenney, the promising young assistant attorney general who resigned rather than prosecute a phony case, finds herself similarly iced out of government work. Ed Cisowski, the state police investigator who was vilified for his meticulous investigation of the Brian Dugan confession, takes early retirement. And a couple of the public defenders who apparently worked too diligently on behalf of Cruz and Hernandez are fired by DuPage County and ostracized by their colleagues.

The Establishment's team, on the other hand, is showered with accolades. Edward Kowal, the original judge who tried to shortcut the process with a single trial and wound up spawning six trials instead, is promoted to chief judge. DuPage County State's Attorney Jim Ryan who shrugged off all contradictory evidence and slogged blindly onward was elected and reelected Illinois Attorney General. Tom Knight becomes a federal prosecutor. The lawyer who took over from Mary Brigid Kenney becomes a judge and so does prosecutor Robert Kilander. And Justice James D. Heiple, who characterized Larry Marshall and the law school deans as "a questionable cabal," is named Chief Justice of the Illinois Supreme Court.[39]

The DuPage County power brokers, however, have apparently learned nothing from their odyssey with Rolando Cruz and they continue to shoot themselves in the feet. When they think nobody's looking, they pull Judge Ronald Mehling off the bench as chief of the felony division and demote him to the ranks. The press is flabbergasted. As the *Tribune's* Eric Zorn says: "Wow."[40]

Awash in bad ink, they quickly restore Judge Mehling to his post. They will have to content themselves with just putting a lid on his career.

Mehling's bosses have good reason to be pissed. He ripped the sheet off a coverup that now involves almost everybody in the courthouse. In addition to the prospect of multi-million dollar payouts to Cruz and Hernandez, there is serious talk of actual indictments against the prosecutors themselves.

In the firestorm that follows the spectacular finale in Mehling's courtroom, the public demands an investigation into the state's handling of the Nicarico case and the probe quickly gets out of hand. Somehow in all the confusion a respected Chicago prosecutor gets appointed to head the probe with no strings attached. William Kunkle, the man who sent away serial killer John Wayne Gacey, is given *carte blanche* to dig into the mess.

On December 12, Kunkle calls a press conference to announce his findings. Focusing on the highly questionable "vision" statement and the secret meeting between the prosecutors and Brian Dugan's lawyer, the grand jury has indicted former assistant state's attorney Tom Knight; his assistant, Patrick King; his successor, Robert Kilander; Sheriff's Lieutenants James Montesano and Robert Winkler; and Detectives Dennis Kurzawa and Thomas Vosburgh. Charged with conspiracy to obstruct justice—felony counts that could put them away for years—they are quickly dubbed the "DuPage Seven." No one can remember a courthouse catastrophe on this scale in the state's history.[41]

CHICAGO—MAY, 1997

In the end, Knight, Kilander and the others are acquitted, which comes as a surprise to no one. It is virtually impossible to convince a middle-class jury that state officials would twist the facts to convict an innocent man. What possible reason would they have? Why would they lie? The thought that elected public officials might send a man to his death just to advance their careers is an abyss too deep to contemplate. The remarkable thing is that the DuPage Seven case reached a jury at all.

Today, despite a mountain of evidence to the contrary, officials in DuPage County still insist that Rolando Cruz is guilty and that he was freed on a technicality. They have little choice. If they were to acknowledge the obvious, then the Nicarico family, whose grief they traded on for job approval ratings, might justifiably turn their years of accumulated wrath on the rightful targets.

But the perpetrators of this awful civics lesson will by no means get off unscathed. The real horror they must live with is the knowledge that right after Jeanine Nicarico's murder, they had Brian Dugan in custody on an unrelated charge. If they had simply checked his record, they would have realized that with his history of sex crimes and door kicking, they had the guy. John Sam would surely have put it all together if they had just left him alone.

Instead they focused on political expedience. They let Dugan slip through their fingers and he went on to kill Melissa Ackerman and two other girls, exactly as Detective Sam had predicted.

> *"Abuses of civil liberty in pursuit of saving face are one of the tragic vanities of prosecutorial power in the United States."*
>
> —Franklin E. Zimring, professor of law
> University of California at Berkeley

CHAPTER FOUR

*"No person…shall be compelled in any criminal case to
be a witness against himself…"*
— 5th Amendment to the U.S. Constitution

CHICAGO—MAY, 1987

Flint Taylor and Jeff Haas have been at this for a long,
long time. They mounted the ramparts back in the 1960s
right out of law school. The Vietnam War was then ripping
the country to pieces and Taylor had just arrived from Boston
when he met Haas, the scion of a famous family of Atlanta
attorneys. Forsaking a future of comfort and privilege, they
opened the People's Law Office in a storefront on Halsted
Street and quickly became the local champions of the poor
and defenseless, famed for fighting city hall on behalf of the
disenfranchised. It was hard traveling.[1]

Their lives changed dramatically in the early hours of
December 4, 1969, when one of their clients, 21-year-old
Black Panther Party Chairman Fred Hampton, was executed
by the Chicago police without benefit of a trial—an act that
backfired in a most spectacular fashion. While this kind of
summary judgement certainly wasn't unique in the Windy
City, this time the police tripped up. Since the raid was con-
ducted in absolute secrecy by a special squad from the state
attorney's office, they forgot to notify the local precinct after
they hauled off the bodies. So the crime scene was left
unguarded and all the physical evidence fell into the hands
of Hampton's lawyers.

Instead of a "fifteen-minute shoot-out" as described by
the police, a federal grand jury found it was more like a three-

minute shoot-in. Of the 99 shots traced to police weapons, most were shotgun blasts or machine-gun bullets that ripped through all three bedrooms of the Panther house at waist level. Hampton, however, was killed by a .45 caliber automatic fired into the top of his skull while he was lying in bed.

This untidiness led to criminal indictments of the raiding party, the state's attorney, and the agent in charge of the Chicago FBI office where the raid was planned. All were acquitted—Hampton's death was blamed on poor planning—but the evidence wouldn't go away and neither would the People's Law Office. On behalf of the survivors they filed a wrongful-death suit against the city, the county and the federal government—a formidable task for a bunch of broke storefront lawyers. But tenacity, they say, often trumps arrogance and, despite a total lack of resources and omnipotent adversaries, they took the case all the way to the Supreme Court and back. After thirteen years of legal combat, the city, county, and federal governments finally settled for $1.85 million to the survivors and their relentless attorneys.

While most of their contemporaries have managed to shed the idealism of the '60s, Haas and Taylor have stayed the course, compass locked on the abstract notion of equal justice. Thirty years later, they are still at it. Unfortunately, most of their work still involves allegations of police misconduct. This time the alleged brutality victim is a convicted cop-killer named Andrew Wilson.

Haas' and Taylor's first connection with Andrew Wilson comes in a phone call from the prisoner himself. Wilson claims his confession was tortured out of him. What's more, the Illinois Supreme Court agreed with him and ordered a new trial. The second jury convicted him anyway, even without the confession, but he's still not satisfied. He is suing the city in federal court for $10 million in monetary damages. If he won he wouldn't actually get a dime, of course. Any award would go directly to the police officer's widow. But Wilson, the cop-killer, is standing on principle. He wants the Chicago police to pay for putting a plastic bag over his head, electrodes on his genitals, and a modified curling iron up his ass.

The case is so distasteful that Federal District Judge Brian Duff can't find any attorneys in town who'll touch it. Three other law firms have already run for cover so now the prisoner himself is appealing to the lawyers of last resort—the PLO, as they are known to friends and foes alike.

Hass and Taylor agree to represent Wilson for nothing. Says Taylor, "No matter who you are, you shouldn't be tortured."

CHICAGO—MARCH, 1989

The letter is postmarked from one of the southern suburbs and it's signed, "Ty." It says, "You are on the right track but there's more to it than this. If you want more information, advertise in the *Southtown Economist*."

A tantalizing lead but too late. The Andrew Wilson trial is already underway and it's not looking good. While Taylor, Haas, and co-counsel John Stainthorp have put together an impressive case, Judge Duff's pretrial rulings pulled the rug out from under them. Jeff Haas has already accused Duff in open court of cheerleading for the city and the judge fired back with a barrage of contempt citations.

They're at the end of the line financially, but a letter like this doesn't come along every day. They put an ad in the south suburban paper saying, "Ty: Want more information." Then they head for court with the evidence in hand.

Police brutality cases are almost impossible to prove. The witnesses are government employees who aren't going to testify against each other, and if the prisoner happens to show up beaten to a pulp, he was obviously resisting arrest. But as the Hampton case reminds us, sometimes the ball can take a funny bounce.

Andrew Wilson's claims of torture were corroborated by photographs taken right after his interrogation. They show an interesting pattern of vertical burn marks on his chest, as if he'd been shoved against a steam radiator and held there. The reason these pictures were taken—a rarity in itself—is that Wilson was so badly beaten when he arrived at Cook County Jail that the officer in charge had him photographed to prove that none of this damage occurred after he arrived.

On close inspection, the pictures also reveal a U-shaped pattern of scabs on Wilson's ear lobes like teeth marks of a tiny alligator. For Flint Taylor and his colleagues this is the lynchpin. Wilson claims the police handcuffed him spread-eagled to rings in the wall on either side of the radiator. Then they connected these little spring clips to his ears and hooked him up to a hand-cranked generator. On the witness stand, he described it this way: "It hurts but it stays in your head...and it grinds your teeth...It grinds, constantly grinds, constantly...The pain just stays in your head...and your teeth constantly grinds and grinds and grinds and grinds and grinds and grinds. All my bottom teeth was loose behind that..."[2] The burn marks on his chest, he says, came from the radiator he slammed against when the cops began turning the crank.

"It burned me," says Wilson, "but I didn't even feel it... That radiator...it wouldn't have mattered. That box...took over."

Experts on the subject say it's customary for torture victims to come unglued when they describe the instruments of their debasement and Andrew Wilson is no exception. Cop killer he may be, but he turns to blubber when he starts describing the mechanics of the ordeal. He has to be excused from the witness stand.

When the Illinois Supreme Court saw these photographs three years earlier they ordered Wilson's confession thrown out. They said the evidence showed that Wilson was in fairly good shape when he was arrested at 5:15 a.m. but "when the defendant was taken by police officers to Mercy Hospital sometime after ten o'clock that night he had about fifteen separate injuries on his head, chest, and leg." The inescapable conclusion, they said, is "the defendant suffered his injuries while in police custody..."[3]

The police officers at the defense table, however, are represented by the able and flamboyant William Kunkle—the man who will soon prosecute the DuPage Seven in the Rolando Cruz debacle—and Judge Duff allows Kunkle to turn the trial into a referendum on cop-killing. While the jurors clearly don't like what they're hearing about the cops, they can't bring themselves to rule in favor of a convicted murderer. They are hopelessly deadlocked, black jurors versus white, and Judge Duff orders a new trial.

It's a crushing blow for the People's Law Office since they're operating on their own nickel, but it turns out the timing couldn't be better. They just got an answer to their ad in the *Southtown Economist*.

CHICAGO—APRIL, 1989

From the beginning, Jeff Haas and Flint Taylor suspected that the Andrew Wilson case was just one thread of a larger quilt. If they pulled carefully on that thread they were convinced it would lead to other revelations. They had no idea.

Their anonymous informant is apparently a police officer with intimate knowledge of Area 2 Headquarters where the interrogation took place. In his latest letter he advises them to check out a prisoner in Cook County Jail named Melvin Jones. Jones, he says, was forced to confess to a different crime by the same crew that would interrogate Andrew Wilson nine days later.

When the PLO lawyers interview Jones in the lockup his story is a remarkable mirror of Wilson's. He names the same names. In both incidents the man in charge was Lieutenant Jon Burge, one of the top detectives at Area 2.

Digging into the transcript of Jones's trial, the PLO investigators find everything they're looking for and then some. Seven years earlier Jones had testified on the witness stand that Burge hooked him up to an electrical generator, and when he protested, Burge told him, "You see, it's just me and you...No court and no state are going to take your word against a Lieutenant's word."[4]

There's also a possible reference to other victims. At one point in the transcript Jones says that Lieutenant Burge threatened to give him the same treatment as "Satan" and "Cochise." It doesn't take long to locate Satan and Cochise—both still in prison—and they have similar stories of institutional mayhem at the hands of Lieutenant Burge. What's more, they each know of other guys who say they were tortured in the Area 2 station house. And these men, in turn, know of others. By the time Taylor, Haas and Stainthorp have picked through this explosion of leads, the list has more than 60 names on it. Most of the stories resonate with Andrew Wilson's account right down to the bizarre details. Several men noted that the role of the "good cop" who tried to stop the torture was played by an officer named McWeeney.[5]

But lurking within this list is a horrifying revelation. Ten of these prisoners are on death row. In several cases, the only evidence against them is the confession that Lieutenant

Burge and his men extracted in that little room upstairs at Area 2 Headquarters.

CHICAGO—JANUARY 26, 1990

The *Chicago Reader* is a product of the 1960s, a free weekly paper launched by the same Aquarian impulse that landed the People's Law Office on Halsted Street. It has survived and prospered in Chicago's cutthroat news market by doing the kind of digging the major dailies won't take time for. The issue that hit the stands this morning leads with a photo of the old brick police station at 91st and Cottage Grove over the headline:

"HOUSE OF SCREAMS"

The article by staff writer John Conroy, is a devastating catalog of the evidence against Lieutenant Jon Burge, and Conroy's meticulous chronicle of Burge's recent trial in Judge Duff's courtroom makes it clear that something is rotten in Area 2. The jury may have deadlocked but the facts on the table demand a federal investigation, says Conroy. "And what about some of the other men who passed through Area 2 and were convicted of crimes on the basis of confessions given after they allegedly had their testicles stood upon, or bags put over their heads, or cattle prods taken to their genitals? Might they in fact be innocent?"[6]

The *Reader* may not have the circulation of the *Trib* but it reaches people who count. David Fogel, head of the police department's Office of Professional Standards, is a maverick appointed by Harold Washington, the city's first and only black mayor. Fogel is about to leave office but as a parting shot he calls in two of his top investigators and tells them to dig into the Wilson case.

Seven months later the report lands on the superintendent's desk and it paints an ugly picture. In the case of Andrew Wilson, it seems his injuries "were sustained during Wilson's detention in an interview room on the second floor of Area Two Headquarters and ...occurred at the hands of the police and under the sanction of...Lieutenant Jon Burge."

The report then goes on to list the names of fifty other victims who claim they were on the receiving end of the Burge team's extrajudicial investigations. The list is broken down by category of torture—electric shocks to the genitals, suffocation by plastic bag, hoisting by handcuffs, etc.—but the bottom line is unambiguous: "abuse did occur and it was systematic," say the authors. "The type of abuse described was not limited to the usual beating, but went into such esoteric areas as psychological techniques and planned torture...Particular command members were aware of the systematic abuse and perpetuated it either by actively participating...or failing to take any action to bring it to an end."[7]

For Police Superintendent LeRoy Martin, this document is about as welcome as a dead mouse in the punch bowl. For one thing, Martin himself, though unnamed, could be one of those "command members" the report is referring to. In 1983 he was a supervisor in Area 2. Jon Burge was one of his officers.

Martin decides to file the report in the bottom drawer and there it stays for a year. But leaks and rumors keep ramping up the pressure. Martin, about to retire himself, decides to contain the damage by throwing a bone to his critics. In the final months of 1991 he issues an order suspending Lieutenant Burge and two of his officers without pay. But this move triggers a formal police board hearing and the existence of the OPS report can no longer be covered up. The city attorneys do their best to suppress it but Federal Judge Milton Shadur sides with Flint Taylor and his colleagues: the report is public property.

In the media firestorm that follows, the city attorneys, still squaring off against the PLO in the Wilson case, opt for a fundamental change in the game plan. For several years they have been maintaining that Lieutenant Burge is innocent of any crime. Now they say he's obviously guilty—and guilty of an offense so heinous that the city couldn't possibly have anything to do with it. After the police board votes to dismiss Burge, the city's counsel sends him a letter saying he's on his own. Since he clearly acted outside established authority, the city is not responsible for any damages and will not indemnify him.

It's a strategy both bold and chilling. Since Lieutenant Burge has no assets, it means the PLO attorneys would never get a dime for their years of work. It would also insure that no lawyer in his right mind would ever get involved with any of these other cases, thus closing the door on the whole sordid business.

CHICAGO—JULY, 1996

It's a nice try, but Judge Gettleman won't go for it. The Andrew Wilson case is now on its third trip through federal court. Judge Robert Gettleman has taken over from Judge Duff and he dismisses the city's argument out of hand. And after examining the police department's own investigation, he sees no reason for a third trial. He enters a summary judgement against the police and the City of Chicago. There's outrage in city hall but the U.S. Seventh Circuit upholds Gettleman's decision, saying the police department's defense "borders on the frivolous."[8]

By the time the city finally pays up—more than $1 million in the end—Lieutenant Burge has been safely retired to Florida so Chicago essentially washes its hands of the whole

business. The daily press, focused on the Wilson case, does-
n't bother to investigate any of the other claims of tortured
confessions. The fact that ten of these men are still awaiting
execution seems of little interest to anybody.

Aaron Patterson, Stanley Howard and Madison Hobley
are among those of the "Death Row Ten" who might be completely innocent of the crimes they confessed to. As Aaron
Patterson says, "Yes, I did some things. But I didn't do this."

Patterson was arrested on April 30, 1986 for murdering
a south side couple who fenced stolen goods. Well known to
the police, he was a top honcho of the Apache Rangers, an
offshoot of one of the city's most violent street gangs.
Unfortunately there was no physical evidence linking him to
the crime. The fingerprints weren't his. The footprints
weren't his. The only witness who fingered him, a teenage
girl, later recanted, saying she'd been threatened by the cops.
But Lieutenant Burge somehow managed to get Aaron
Patterson to confess.

The hangup, once again, was a photograph. Burge and
his men made the mistake of leaving Patterson alone in the
interrogation room when they were done with him.
Handcuffed to his seat, he found a paperclip on the floor and
scratched a note into the back of the bench:

"AARON 4/30 I LIE ABOUT MURDERS. POLICE
THREATEN ME WITH VIOLENCE. SLAPPED AND SUF-
FOCATED ME WITH PLASTIC."[9]

The photograph of the message was taken four weeks
later under a court order from the public defender's office.

The judge in Patterson's capital murder trial refused to
let the jury hear any of this evidence, fearing no doubt it
would color their view of the confession. So Patterson took
to yelling in court that he had been tortured and this upset

the judge and jury alike. Patterson was convicted and sentenced to death in 1989. But the photograph still exists, and with his interrogator now an acknowledged torturer, those paperclip scratchings on the back of the bench are taking on new significance.

Claims of torture from a second death row inmate, Stanley Howard, are supported by medical records. A stickup artist on the run, Howard was captured in a wild chase, then taken to the hospital where he was treated for minor injuries. Back at the station house, he confessed to murdering an innocent man who was just sitting in his car with a girlfriend. After the confession they had to take Howard back to the hospital and his second exam listed a whole new set of injuries that matched his description of the interrogation.

What lends credence to Howard's claim of innocence is the rest of the evidence. The victim and his girlfriend were having an affair—both were married to other people—and for a clandestine get together, they picked an awful spot—right around the corner from the woman's apartment.

Several people in the building heard an argument just before the gunshot and it didn't sound like a confrontation between a stickup man and a total stranger. It sounded like a fight between two people who knew each other.

"I told you I'd get you," says the male voice.

"Don't hurt him," shouts the woman. "Just take me home."

"POP!"

None of this information made it into the trial. It was simply disallowed. The judge, a former policeman from Area 2, found it impossible to believe that the officers would torture someone to get a statement. He refused to suppress the confession and in 1987 Howard was convicted and sentenced to die.

Despite the Burge revelations, a comprehensive review of all these cases continues to meet with resistance from the courts. Judges, quite understandably, are loathe to take the word of convicted felons over sworn officers of the law. But at least one of the judges may have had a private agenda in bringing down the hammer. Darrell Cannon is another death row inmate who claims that three of these officers put a shotgun in his mouth, addressed him as "nigger," pulled down his pants and shocked his testicles with a cattle prod. His claim was casually dismissed by Judge Thomas Maloney, but perhaps for selfish reasons. Judge Maloney was later stripped of his robes and sent to the Big House for fifteen years when an FBI sting revealed that he had been fixing murder trials for as little as $10,000. If you didn't pay up, the judge would give you both barrels. Since he was running his courtroom as a business, he had to come down heavily on non-paying customers like Cannon in order to maintain his tough law-and-order image. As Professor Larry Marshall said at the time, "if a judge is in the business of selling acquittals, he will not be giving them away for free—even to those who deserve them."

As the decade wears on, revelations of Byzantine scandals in the Illinois criminal justice system continue to surface with triphammer regularity. But some of the most chilling disclosures are yet to come—not at the hands of professional investigators but from a bunch of amateurs—college students in search of extra credit.

CHICAGO—AUGUST, 1998

Since Larry Marshall was sucked into the Rolando Cruz case in 1990 he has been drawn ever deeper into the swamp of capital punishment litigation. The man he's trying to save at the moment is a 43-year-old African American named

Anthony Porter. Porter has an I.Q. of 51. If the state proceeds with his execution it will break the record currently held by Alabama which executed a man with an I.Q. of 56. An I.Q. of 100 is normal. Less than 70 is considered retarded. Porter is said to have the intellectual capacity of a 4th grader.

To people like Marshall this amounts to the execution of children. Although the Supreme Court ruled in 1989 that juveniles under 15 cannot die at the hands of the government, they found nothing inherently unconstitutional about executing adults who are the mental equivalent of juveniles. So it's up to the states, and of the 38 that allow the death penalty, only a dozen have outlawed it for the mentally retarded. Illinois is not one of those states, so Marshall has joined the Porter legal team in a last ditch effort to get a stay from the state supreme court. Innocence isn't the issue here. The question is whether Porter is intelligent enough to be executed. Does he understand what's going on?

They have pulled everybody into one room at the Northwestern University Law School to make sure they've covered all the bases. Along with the law students, volunteers, lawyers and investigators, there is a Northwestern journalism professor named David Protess who decided at the last minute to pop in and get an overview of the case. This will prove to be the luckiest day of Anthony Porter's life.

David Protess teaches investigative journalism the old fashioned way: learn by doing. A professor at Northwestern University's Medill School of Journalism, Protess became internationally famous in 1996 when his students, as a class project, freed four men from death row by proving their innocence. All the students got "A"s.

The case of the "Ford Heights Four" was a chilling echo of the Cruz-Hernandez debacle in nearby DuPage County, parallel both in time and prosecutorial double-dealing. Like the rape and murder of little Jeanine Nicarico, this was a "heater case" with press and public in full cry. A young white couple, just engaged, was kidnapped from a filling station in the white suburb of Homewood and their bodies were found in an abandoned townhouse in the adjacent black neighborhood of East Chicago Heights. The girl had been repeatedly raped, then she and her fiancé were shot in the head.

With vengeance in the air the Cook County Sheriff's Police fixed their sights on the first suspects they came across, then they twisted a few arms and fabricated a few facts just to make sure these monsters got what they deserved. Like the DuPage County prosecutors, once they were committed to this course of action they were ill-prepared to face any conflicting evidence. So when it showed up they buried it.

As with Cruz and Hernandez, the Ford Heights Four went through a cascade of trials and in this case the state's key witness was a mentally deficient teenager. When she recanted her trial testimony, the state threw her in prison for perjury, and when she went back to the original story they let her out. Reclusive, uncooperative, the woman refused to be interviewed—until one day in 1998 when these three white girls from Northwestern University showed up.

She looked at them and decided it was time to tell all. It seems she'd had a dream the night before. In the dream some white girls had knocked on her door. They had come to talk about the case of the Ford Heights Four.

Within days the woman was in front of the Channel 5 TV cameras with a tale of jackboot justice. She said the police and prosecutors had coached her on exactly what to say and had threatened to take her children and throw her in prison if she didn't follow the script. This version of the story had a certain resonance since they had indeed taken her children and thrown her in prison when she recanted and kept her there for seven years until she changed her tune to re-sync with the prosecution.

The students, inflamed by what they were uncovering, were further dismayed by the discovery that a police informant had named the real killers within days of the crime. Unfortunately this information had come too late—the case was already on rails.

Meanwhile, the Ford Heights legal team was demanding that the new science of DNA matching be applied to the semen sample taken from the dead girl's body. The state flatly refused, but when their star witness showed up on television saying the whole case was built on a lie, the prosecutors could hold out no longer.

The DNA tests were agreed to and the results swept the state's case into the trash. The semen sample did not match any of the Ford Heights prisoners. After 18 years in prison, all four were exonerated and released.

These stunning revelations turned Protess and his students into instant media stars complete with book deals and urgent calls from Hollywood. His critics now call him a shameless self-promoter who has crossed the line between journalism and advocacy but if that's the worst they can come up with in the light of the powerful enemies he's accumulating, he must be a choirboy.

When Protess was first approached about the Porter case in August he was inclined to pass. First of all there's no time. The execution is set for September. Second, he figures the guy is probably guilty so the real issue is whether he's retarded. But after the meeting with Porter's defense team he decides to include Porter among the possible cases to be considered when the next class meets.

"What you need to know," he tells the students, "is that if you take that case, the stakes are going to be high, the pressure intense. There are some rich questions as to his competency and even whether he committed the crime, but I don't know whether he's guilty or not. You will have to find that out. You will also have to keep in mind one other thing. Anthony Porter could be dead before you reach your first final."

He usually gives his students three weeks to decide if they want to be involved with a particular case. This time they've got three days.

CHICAGO—AUGUST, 1998

Anthony Porter was convicted of murdering a young man and woman in the bleachers of a South Side swimming pool on an August night in 1982. A convicted armed robber, gang banger, and all-around pain in the ass, he was immediately a prime suspect. There was never any physical evidence but there was an eyewitness named William Taylor who placed Porter at the scene with gun in hand.

The fault lines in these cases are usually buried somewhere in the original police files and the advantage the students have is the patience to sift this material for the nuggets that seem to elude the professionals. The tip will usually be some minor detail. Like the fact that eyewitness William Taylor said Porter had the gun in his left hand. Porter is right-handed.

Curious about what is not in the reports, the students track down the dead girl's mother. They discover that this woman was saying from the outset that Anthony Porter was not the killer. She says her daughter left for the park that night with her fiancé and a couple they knew as Margaret and Alstory Simon. She never saw her daughter alive again but a few hours later Simon and his common-law wife packed up and left town in a rush and were never seen again.

Until this moment the whole legal effort has been focused on Porter's I.Q. Now they realize he may actually be innocent. And they are out of time.

CHICAGO—SEPTEMBER 21, 1998

To put a kinder face on the mechanics of execution, Illinois has abandoned the old electric chair at Stateville in favor of lethal injections in the modern surgical chamber downstate at Tamms. The new gurney, unfortunately, with its arm restraints extending out on either side, looks uncomfortably like a cross. Anthony Porter will be the first man to try it out. His date with the needle is three days away.

Porter's jailers graciously ask what he'd like for his last meal but the guards on death row tend to be unsympathetic. They remind him that in a few hours he'll be "blue meat" himself.

In Springfield his lawyers are fighting for a stay. They've hired an expert neuropsychologist who has just interviewed the prisoner. He describes Porter as "a behaviorally disordered 10-year-old." In Illinois an inmate has to at least understand his punishment before he can be put to death. The doctor wants more time for a full evaluation.

The prosecutors believe Porter is faking it but given their recent track record they decide not to stand in the way. With 50 hours to spare, the Illinois Supreme Court grants a temporary stay. The lower court has six weeks to decide if Anthony Porter is able to understand what's about to happen to him.

In their latest brief, Porter's lawyers mention almost in passing that in addition to mental incompetence there may be evidence of actual innocence as well. These claims, however, have been so thoroughly rehashed over the last 16 years that nobody pays any attention.

CHCAGO—NOVEMBER, 1998

It's freezing cold and the swimming pool is empty but the bleachers are still intact and everything else is pretty much as it was that summer night sixteen years ago. Protess's students have come to the scene of the crime in Washington Park to reconstruct the shooting. Working from court records and police reports, they put the various players into position. The first thing they notice is that if the key prosecution witness, William Taylor, was standing where he said he was, he would not have been able to ID the shooter on the other side of the fence in the darkness at the far end of the pool. According to Taylor's testimony, the shooter then ran past him heading for the far exit. That makes no sense. Why would the gunman run the length of the pool—under the lights and past a witness—instead of ducking out that exit right next to him?

They also find a red flag in the original police report. When Taylor was first interviewed he said he didn't see the shooter. After an all-night session at the station house he named Porter.

CHICAGO—DECEMBER 14, 1998

If you spotted Paul Ciolino in a West Side saloon—heavyset, street-wise, hawk-eyed—you'd immediately peg him as a cop. These days he's a private investigator who serves as mentor and bodyguard for the Protess team when they venture into terra incognita, which, for the average white college kid, includes half the city.

Working the South Side they locate William Taylor, the only person who testified to having seen Porter shoot the two victims. When Ciolino and the students confront him with the flaws in his testimony Taylor finally admits that he lied on the witness stand. "I didn't see Anthony Porter," he says. "I didn't see anybody."[10]

In what is becoming a grindingly familiar refrain, he says the cops threatened him and told him what to say. He was beside the pool putting on his clothes, he says, when he heard the shots, and the cops forced him to say it was Porter. He says one officer kept asking him, "Who are you more afraid of? Porter—or us?"

DANVILLE CORRECTIONAL CENTER— JANUARY 8, 1999

Like a bowling ball curling in for the strike, Protess's investigation is about to pulverize the state's case. On the trail of Alstory Simon, the mystery man who vanished after the murder, the team tracks down a nephew who was living with Simon at the time. He's in prison on an unrelated case. He says his uncle, a drug dealer, told him that night he was going to see the two victims, then he "returned to the apartment...took me aside and told me that he had 'taken care of Jerry and Marilyn.'"[11] The next morning, he says, the family threw everything in the car and took off for Milwaukee and never came back.

MILWAUKEE—JANUARY 27, 1999

A tip from the nephew leads to other relatives and within a week the investigators have located Inez Jackson, the estranged wife of the suspected shooter. Two female students make the initial approach and like magic they get Inez to agree to meet the professor. A couple of days later they pick her up and take her to a restaurant where Protess and

Paul Ciolino are waiting. They have a message for Inez from her nephew. He wants her to tell the whole story.

Like a volcano waiting to erupt, she unloads. She says the gunman was her husband, Alstory Simon, who had a beef with the other guy over a drug debt. She says they've been separated for six years but she didn't come forward because she was afraid of what he might do to her or the children. But she's glad the students found her. "Now," she says, "maybe I can sleep at night."

In her retelling there is one riveting detail that sheds some light on the sand in the gears of the criminal justice system. The morning after the murder, just before they blew town, Inez heard a knock at the door. It was the police. She knew the cops had spotted them in the park so they had to be suspects. She figured the jig was up. But instead of an interrogation, the detectives showed them a mug shot and asked if they would confirm that Porter was the shooter. "They told me who did it," says Inez Jackson. "I didn't have a chance to say nothing because they didn't ask me nothing."

MILWAUKEE—FEBRUARY 3, 1999

Alstory Simon doesn't want to talk about it. He recently did four years for armed robbery and he's not interested in going back to the joint. He's aware of the fact that his estranged wife has been saying terrible things about him on television, but he won't crack. Then Paul Ciolino, the ex-cop, shows Simon a video. It's a tape of a heretofore unknown eyewitness and he identifies Simon as the trigger-man. The tape in fact is a fake—the guy on screen is Ciolino's pal—and Simon isn't that stupid. But when he stops the tape, there's Inez on the evening news saying he did it. Convinced now the police are closing in on him he begins babbling about how it was all self defense, that he thought the other guy was going for a gun, that the thing with the woman was an accident—

Ciolino tells him that the way to make sure his side of the story gets out is to put it on videotape. Simon says okay. Ciolino breaks out the camera.

COOK COUNTY JAIL—FEBRUARY 3, 1999

Despite Anthony Porter's alleged incompetence, he has no trouble understanding the implications when a reporter breaks the news that Alstory Simon has confessed. He sinks to a stool in the visiting room, then looks skyward and shouts, "Hallelujah!" with tears streaming down his face.

If he was indeed faking his mental limitations it was the performance of a lifetime. Without that little tiff over his I.Q. he would have been dead four months ago. But on February 6, 1999, Anthony Porter, once scheduled to be the 12th inmate to die in Illinois since the death penalty was reinstated, becomes instead the 10th inmate to walk off Illinois' death row alive.

> "It is now common knowledge that in the early- to mid-1980s, Chicago Police Commander Jon Burge and many of the officers working under him regularly engaged in the physical abuse and torture of prisoners to extract confessions."
> —U.S. District Judge Milton Shadur[12]

> "It's kind of like an amazing disgrace."
> —Tim Lohraff, People's Law Office

CHAPTER FIVE

"No person shall be… deprived of life, liberty, or property, without due process of law…"
—5th Amendment to the U.S. Constitution

CHICAGO—NOVEMBER, 1998

Moses Harrison II has decided he's not going to have anything to do with capital punishment anymore. That is significant because he's on the Illinois Supreme Court. "The system is not working," writes Justice Harrison. "Innocent people are being sentenced to death. If these men dodged the executioner, it was only because of luck and the dedication of the attorneys, reporters, family members, and volunteers….They survived despite the criminal justice system, not because of it…One must wonder how many others have not been so fortunate."[1]

Justice Harrison's broadside gets everybody's attention and the timing is auspicious. It serves as a curtain-raiser for the amazing drama to follow. And though the State of Illinois will take center stage in these events, the fallout will indict us all.

NORTHWESTERN UNIVERSITY— NOVEMBER, 1998

A year ago Larry Marshall went to a legislative hearing in Springfield where he watched five former death row inmates tell the lawmakers about their experience at the hands of the state. What got his attention was their affect on the crowd. "Just five of them sitting at one table had an amazing impact on the audience," says Marshall. "It dawned on me that bringing together everyone who'd been exonerated all over the country would be a great way to illustrate how innocent people will be sentenced to death and killed if we don't do something."[2]

He dispatched a brigade of law students and volunteers to sift news archives, court records and phone directories looking for the 74 men and women who belong to this exclusive club. After a nationwide search they managed to locate over half the roster and somehow they have convinced 30 of them to show up in Chicago in the dead of winter.

On November 13, "Life After Death Row: The First National Conference on Wrongful Convictions and the Death Penalty" opens at the Northwestern University Law School to a sellout crowd of 1,200 lawyers and activists. It exceeds anything Marshall and his colleagues expected. At the podium are the torchbearers who've been leading the death penalty opposition over the last three decades—Stephen Bright of the Southern Center for Human Rights, Brian Stevenson of the Equal Justice Initiative in Alabama, and the venerable Anthony Amsterdam of New York University Law School, the attorney who got the death penalty declared unconstitutional in 1972.

But the assembly on stage takes the focus—30 men and women staring back at the audience with a mixture of rage, bitterness, hostility and forgiveness. Society has played the ultimate trick on these people—stealing their youth and leading them to the jaws of death only to say, "just kidding." The fact that 30 of them are still willing to help save us from ourselves seems oddly reassuring.

In addition to the local celebrities—Rolando Cruz and the Ford Heights defendants—there are national figures here as well. Rubin "Hurricane" Carter, the professional boxer whose New Jersey murder conviction was derailed, in part, by Bob Dylan, and Randall Dale Adams who was rescued from death row by a film crew that exposed his story in the 1988 documentary *The Thin Blue Line*. Adams was convicted in a Texas lynching so embroiled in prosecutorial misconduct that his lawyer quit the bar in revulsion after the trial. Adams, in his late twenties at the time, was fingered as a cop killer by David Harris, the 16-year-old he'd hitched a ride with. A considerable body of evidence pointed to Harris as the real killer, but the Dallas prosecutors buried it and then made deals with the witnesses to lock down the case against Adams.

Looking over the record of this travesty it seems incredible that the prosecutors fixed on Adams when the facts clearly supported his version of events and not Harris's. Why would they go after Adams instead of the real killer? The only obvious explanation is profoundly unsettling. Randall Dale Adams was over 17 and therefore eligible for the death penalty. Somebody had to die for killing that cop and Harris was too young.

On the Northwestern Law School stage the living ghosts prove irresistible to the TV cameras exactly as Larry Marshall expected. And as the image of these once-desperate faces hits the nightly news, it's impossible to ignore the fact that most of the faces are black. But black or white, it is timing they have in common, for under the present rules of the game many of them would already be six feet under. "There are states right now that are trying to make the death penalty process much swifter," says Marshall, "even though the average time it took for the people at our conference to be exonerated was seven years. What that means is, if you insist that you want to have a death penalty that kills people in five years, most of the people at the conference would have been dead by the time the evidence of their innocence emerged."

The emotional climax of the conference comes on the

third day as the victims themselves line up to take the podium. "My name is Joseph Burrows. The State of Illinois sought to kill me for a murder I did not commit...." "My name is Dale Johnston.... Had the State of Ohio gotten its way I would be dead today...." "My name is Shabakah Brown. The State of Florida sought to kill me for a murder I did not commit..." "...had the State of Alabama gotten its way I would be dead today...." "...I would be dead today...." "...I would be dead today...."

As they parade across the stage to the beat of African drums the audience stands and applauds, for they are modern-day gladiators who have survived the deadliest contest we could devise. As NYU's Anthony Amsterdam says, "This is a powerful moment in the history of conscience."

The last person to reach the podium is a slight middle-aged woman who spent her youth on death row in Florida. Her date with oblivion was arranged by false witnesses, jailhouse snitches, a plea bargain with the actual killer and exculpatory evidence that was hidden by the prosecutor. In her knit sweater and rimless glasses, she could be the school librarian.

"My name is Sonja Jacobs. The State of Florida sought to kill me for a murder I did not commit. I was sentenced to death in 1976 and was released in 1992. Had the State of Florida gotten its way I would be dead today."

They applaud but she's not finished.

"My daughter's father, Jesse Tafero, was not as lucky as I was." She struggles to go on. "By the time evidence of our innocence was exposed, the State of Florida had already executed him."

CHICAGO—JANUARY, 1999

One of the century's most notorious snapshots of journalistic hubris shows President Harry Truman holding up the

Chicago Tribune on the morning of his 1948 re-election. The headline says: "DEWEY WINS"—a sensational exercise in wishful thinking that the *Tribune* has never lived down. But the paper suffered an even more humbling lapse in 1969 following the death of Black Panther leader Fred Hampton.

Immediately after the pre-dawn raid on Hampton's apartment, serious questions were raised about the official version of events. The police defended their actions by providing the *Tribune* with exclusive photographs of the crime scene that proved the Panthers had fired at them. The photos showed bullet holes in the back door and door frame coming from inside the apartment. Even more telling was a bedroom door riddled with bullet holes that clearly showed the Panthers had fired through that door at police. The *Tribune's* front-page exclusive blew the Panthers' version out of the water and confirmed everything the police had said.

But since the cops had somehow failed to seal the crime scene, reporters from the *Chicago Sun-Times* went out to the Panther apartment on West Monroe Street and found that the "bullet holes" in the back porch were in fact nail heads and chipped paint. The bedroom door did indeed have bullet holes that went from the inside to the outside, but these holes lined up perfectly with bullet holes in the wall, which meant the door was standing open during the raid. The bullet holes came from police weapons fired through the wall from the living room.

The *Chicago Tribune* masthead used to say, "World's Greatest Newspaper," and the management does not take ridicule lightly, especially at the hands of the *Sun-Times*. In the paint-peeling inquest that followed, the editors discovered that their veteran police reporter was in bed with the cops and he simply went for their version, hook, line, and sinker. This led to a shakeup that fundamentally altered the paper's relationship with local law enforcement and by all accounts the World's Greatest Newspaper has done its best to steer clear of that trap ever since. If there is any lingering doubt, it is about to be dispelled.

For the past two years, an investigative team led by *Tribune* reporters Ken Armstrong and Maurice Possley has been cruising the back alleys of the Illinois criminal justice system trying to make sense of the courtroom disasters that have been surfacing like clockwork. After digging through the history of some 5,000 cases they have come to the conclusion that it's sometimes hard to tell the good guys from the bad guys.[3]

On Sunday, January 10, the first installment of a five-part series opens on page one and it is a compendium of evil—extortion, deception, bribery, perjury—not on the part of the accused but on behalf of the state. Over the next five days the series rips the sheet off the unseen world of prosecutorial misconduct and wraps up with an indictment of the whole profession.

The problem, according to the *Tribune* investigators, is structural. Winning is rewarded. Cheating goes unpunished: "In an environment where prosecutors recite conviction rates like boxers touting won-loss records, the risks are negligible for those who break the rules of a fair trial."[4]

Armstrong and Possley found that over the last four decades some 380 homicide convictions nationwide—67 of them death penalties—were thrown out because the prosecutors were caught covering up evidence of innocence or presenting evidence they knew was false. This kind of deception is so reprehensible that the U.S. Supreme Court has said that it calls for criminal charges and disbarment. But nobody seems to be taking the high court seriously. "Not one of those prosecutors was ever convicted of a crime or barred from practicing law. Instead many saw their careers advance, becoming judges or district attorneys. One became a congressman."[5]

And that is the unnerving motif in the *Tribune* revelations. They found that the more outrageous a prosecutor's behavior, the more likely he or she is to move up the ladder: "In Georgia, George "Buddy" Darden became a congressman after a court concluded that he withheld evidence in a case where seven men, later exonerated, were convicted of murder and one was sentenced to death." A New York prosecutor managed to win murder convictions against a couple of African-American men by concealing an eyewitness report that said the killers were white. Despite this unprincipled quest to win at any cost, the prosecutor became a judge.

State's attorneys in South Carolina, Arizona, Colorado, Illinois and Indiana were caught hiding evidence—pistols, pipes, and knives found on the victims—in order to undermine claims of self-defense. A Florida man, convicted of poisoning his own children, was freed after the prosecutor's secretary discovered evidence of the man's innocence buried in her boss's filing cabinet. She told her boyfriend, he boosted the files and passed them on to muckraking journalist Mark Lane, who blew the whistle. In New Jersey—always a contender whatever the title—prosecutors concealed evidence that their star witness was the real killer.

"Winning has become more important than doing justice," says Harvard law professor Alan Dershowitz. "Nobody runs for the Senate saying I did justice."[6]

What makes this malfeasance so routine is the fact that you can get away with it. In a nationwide search of court records, the *Tribune* reporters were amazed to find only two prosecutors who were ever nailed on criminal charges for this kind of courtroom legerdemain. Both cases were downgraded to misdemeanors. They were fined $500.[7]

The rewards for ruthless prosecution, however, are well documented. Cook County prosecutor Patrick Quinn had two cases thrown out on appeal in 1997 because he broke the basic rules of fairness, but by the time the Illinois Appellate Court chastened him it was irrelevant. Quinn had become a member of the Appellate Court himself.[8]

Then there is Cook County prosecutor Scott Arthur, one of the men who convicted the "Ford Heights Four" and sent two innocent men to death row.[9] "Smart, blunt and frequently profane, Arthur intimidated defense lawyers, steam rolled judges and won over juries."[10] He was, in short, a bully, but his workaholic pace and outstanding conviction rate caught the attention of State's Attorney Richard M. Daley, who was then concentrating on his campaign for mayor.

Even as the appeals courts were castigating Arthur for his callous disregard of the rights of defendants, Daley made him a supervisor. And six months after the Illinois Supreme Court blasted him for destroying the courtroom's "aura of dignity" with personal attacks on everyone including the judge, Daley named him head of the felony trial division. Though his convictions were reversed by higher courts more often than almost anybody in the office, Arthur was then assigned to monitor and counsel other prosecutors who were facing misconduct charges.

There has been no attempt to remedy this judicial cancer and in fact things are heading in the opposite direction. It's no longer possible to sue a prosecutor for damages in civil court because they are literally above the law. In 1976, the U.S. Supreme Court granted prosecutors total immunity from lawsuits even if they conceal evidence or knowingly use false evidence. The court's argument was that there are plenty of other checks on misconduct since prosecutors can be disbarred or indicted. That turns out to be a hollow threat.

The *Tribune* search failed to turn up a single prosecutor who was disbarred for this kind of treachery.

The high court also assumes that prosecutors are answerable to the voters on election day. That might be true if the voters had any idea what the prosecutors are up to but it's virtually impossible to find out. On those occasions when the appellate court does tear into some state's attorney for outrageous conduct, chances are nobody will ever find out. When the opinion is published, the name of the offending counsel will usually be omitted as a matter of professional courtesy. And if the prosecutor should be named for some reason, the court may dispose of the case with an "unpublished order," an opinion that goes into the files but doesn't show up in the law books or the electronic databases. For all practical purposes, it doesn't exist. The *Tribune* discovered that the Illinois Appellate Court is now disposing of 90 percent of its criminal cases in unpublished orders.[11]

This professional discretion is understandable. Prosecutors, judges and lawyers are all in the same club and nobody likes a snitch. But as Armstrong and Possley remind us, "Prosecutors are the criminal justice system's gatekeepers. They hold powers and responsibilities unique in American society. The decisions they make can determine who avoids or stands trial, who is convicted or acquitted, who lives or dies."[12]

SPRINGFIELD—FEBRUARY, 1999

When Anthony Porter is freed from death row it sends a jolt through the state's legal establishment unlike anything that's gone before. Porter is unquestionably innocent— another man, Alstory Simon, confessed to the crime on videotape—but Porter had reached the point of selecting his last meal before he was exonerated. This narrow squeak is profoundly disturbing to people who had convinced themselves this sort of thing was impossible.

A spokesman for Governor George Ryan, trying to put the best face on all this, says the Porter case proves the system works—he was ultimately found innocent. But the governor quickly distances himself from this doublespeak. "I'm not sure the system worked," says Ryan. A former pharmacist from Kankakee, the Governor is a conservative Republican and by all accounts a decent man. He believes in the death penalty, he campaigned for it, but now he's the guy who actually signs the death warrant and this close call with Anthony Porter was unnerving. "I think everybody understands what's at stake here," he says. "An innocent man was about to die, and thank God he didn't."[13]

Even law-and-order Attorney General Jim Ryan (no relation) is having second thoughts. So is mayor Richard M. Daley. The fact that all these rabid death-penalty politicians are heading for cover is simply a reflection of what's already obvious to their constituents. They have created a system that relies on student volunteers to keep it from killing innocent people.

CHICAGO—MARCH, 1999

When Governor Ryan is in Chicago he works out of the Thompson Center, a skyscraper at the edge of the Loop, and this morning the plaza in front of the building is filled with 500 well-dressed protesters. Among these unlikely radicals is a former Supreme Court justice, a former U.S. Senator and a former White House counsel. They're pressing the governor to declare a moratorium on executions.

At the head of this parade, of course, is Professor Larry Marshall and he senses that the tide is turning. "When Richard Daley is calling for a moratorium, things have changed. It's not just a fringe issue anymore."[14]

Seven days later Marshall's assessment is affirmed in an open letter to Governor Ryan signed by over 300 of the state's top lawyers. Authored by one of the solons of the University of Chicago Law School, it reads, "The system we care deeply about suffers with every new accusation that possible police misconduct, prosecutorial abuse or inept defense has produced the wrongful conviction and death sentence of an innocent person. We shudder at such charges."[15]

Ryan, a staunch death penalty advocate, rejects the idea of a moratorium, but he was clearly shaken by the near miss with Anthony Porter. Ryan's spokesman admits that the subject is on the table.

CHICAGO—MAY, 1999

Ronald Jones claimed from the beginning that his confession was beaten out of him in a South Side police station. That allegation was never taken seriously and Jones wound up on death row for the 1985 murder and rape of a Chicago woman. But by 1994, the science of DNA matching had advanced so dramatically that even microscopic bits of tissue and semen could be tested and Jones's lawyer, Richard Cunningham, thought his DNA might exonerate him.

At the hearing, Cook County Judge John Morrissey practically laughed Cunningham out of the courtroom. "What issue could possibly be resolved by DNA testing?" asked Judge Morrissey.[16] The lawyers then dragged the prosecutors kicking and screaming all the way to the state supreme court. The high court finally cleared the way for the tests—which proved conclusively that the semen found on the victim's body could not have come from Ronald Jones.

Instead of instant exoneration, Jones remained in prison. The prosecutors were insisting they were going to retry him, but the press was skeptical. *Tribune* columnist Eric

Zorn warned them not to try any "prosecutorial gymnastics I call the 'Full Twisting DuPage'—radically changing the theory of the crime in light of exculpatory evidence in order to preserve a conviction."

For the last twenty-two months the state has tried to come up with some explanation for Jones's confession that doesn't point the finger at police brutality, but on May 17 they finally throw in the towel. After eight years on ice, Ronald Jones is at last unshackled—the 12th inmate to walk off Illinois' death row alive.[17]

CHICAGO—NOVEMBER, 1999

The specter of killing an innocent man has suddenly become tangible. People who never gave it a second thought are beginning to ask questions. After 25 years of solid public support, polls are showing uneasiness among the electorate and the debate that has long been confined to academics and activists is about to hit the front pages. To move it along, *Tribune* reporter Ken Armstrong—teamed this time with reporter Steve Mills—has been working for the last eight months on a follow up to the paper's January salvo at the prosecutors. Armstrong and Mills have looked into every capital punishment file since the penalty was restored in Illinois 22 years ago—285 cases in all—and if anyone was expecting good news it is dispelled by the headline on November 14: "The Failure of the Death Penalty in Illinois —Part One."

The series opens with a scathing indictment of the whole criminal justice system. "The findings reveal a system so plagued by unprofessionalism, imprecision and bias...a system so riddled with faulty evidence, unscrupulous trial tactics and legal incompetence that justice has been forsaken."

After this ringing endorsement it's all down hill. Armstrong and Mills find the bungling and deception so pervasive that fully half the death-penalty cases appealed to the Illinois Supreme Court are sent back for a new trial or sentencing hearing.

Among the most sinister flaws is the use of jailhouse informants. A third of the Illinois inmates exonerated from death row were originally put there by snitch testimony, evidence that some states consider so unreliable it's outlawed.

Armstrong and Mills tell of a prolific L.A. jailhouse informant named Vernon White who once gave police a demonstration of how to fabricate an instant confession. "Using a jail telephone, White—a convicted kidnapper, robber and car thief—posed as a police officer, prosecutor and bail bondsman to obtain information about a murder suspect he had never met, then falsified jail records to show he had shared a cell with the suspect."

The average informant, however, doesn't need to be nearly this inventive because the police may simply pass on the necessary details themselves. But from time to time there are practitioners of the snitch art who rise to such prominence that state's attorneys are practically bidding for their services. One of the most remarkable is a sometime coke dealer named Big Daddy Woo Woo—a.k.a. Tommy Dye, etc.—who helped convict so many people that he was practically running a one-man railroad to the Big House.

Dye is a favorite of Cook County prosecutors, developing confessions in three major cases and putting one man on death row. Two of the men he helped put away claim that Dye rifled their prison records while they were out of the cell, then used the information to manufacture confessions. True or not, there's no denying Dye himself made out very well from these encounters. His 14-year theft and firearms sentence was cut in half, several other criminal charges were dropped altogether, and he and his girlfriend wound up living off the federal Witness Protection Program.[18]

But Dye apparently forgot where his bread was buttered. In a rare lapse of self-preservation, he stupidly switched sides and testified against the main witness in a federal drug case. The prosecutors had little choice but to attack Dye's credibility so they decided to expose him. Suddenly this witness they had lauded in trial after trial was denounced as a drug dealer, career criminal and admitted perjurer—an "accomplished con artist" with a "nefarious background."

This blistering attack is now part of the court record and it poses something of a problem for the Cook County State's Attorneys because they plan to use Dye in the retrial of the man he helped put on death row. But while Dye is now wanted in Miami for fraud, in Baltimore for auto theft, in Denver for robbery and San Diego for burglary, nobody can lay hands on him. As a special witness, he's under the protection of the Cook County State's Attorney's Office.

The *Tribune* series, after reviewing the dramatic sins of the Ford Heights Four and Rolando Cruz affairs, finally highlights the contrast between the U.S. and Canada by comparing a Cook County homicide case with a similar case in Ontario: "Both were convicted of murder with jailhouse-informant testimony and hair-comparison evidence...both were exonerated by DNA evidence." But when the Canadian prisoner was released, the provincial government appointed a special commission to make sure this kind of thing never happened again. They grilled experts from all over the world and two years later their 1,200-page report recommended severe restrictions on hair evidence and jailhouse snitches. Those recommendations became government policy.

Cook County officials, on the other hand, took the night train. They settled the victim's damage suit out of court, sparing themselves a public airing that might have shed light on the station house beatings, the incompetent lawyers, the official perjury and the courtroom black magic.

CHICAGO—JANUARY 31, 2000

If this were a screenplay it would now call for a scene in which the governor reads the *Tribune* series, then slams his fist on the desk and grabs the phone. And since events in Illinois are now unfolding on a Shakespearean scale, the screenplay is writing itself.

In the floodlit press room at the State of Illinois Building, Governor George Ryan steps to the podium. Acknowledging the impact of the *Tribune* investigation, he says, "I now favor a moratorium because I have grave concerns about our state's shameful record of convicting innocent people and putting them on death row....I cannot support a system which, in its administration, has proven so fraught with error and has come so close to the ultimate nightmare, the state's taking of innocent life...

"Until I can be sure that everyone sentenced to death in Illinois is truly guilty, until I can be sure with moral certainty that no innocent man or woman is facing a lethal injection, no one will meet that fate...."

The Governor says he will not approve another execution until a special commission has examined the capital system's flaws. "This, in effect, is a moratorium."

At least six states have been talking about some kind of action like this but Ryan's decision makes Illinois the first of the country's 38 capital punishment states to formally suspend executions. The fact that he's a Republican death penalty stalwart gives him the footing to stand up to his critics. "How do you prevent another Anthony Porter," he asks, "another innocent man or woman from paying the ultimate penalty for a crime he or she did not commit? Today I cannot answer that question."

Surprisingly, Ryan's leap of faith meets with resounding approval. Nobody accuses him of being soft on crime and fellow legislators from both sides of the aisle seem almost relieved. It's clear that some of these politicians have been waiting for somebody else to jump out of the foxhole. Vermont's Sen. Patrick Leahy calls it "courageous and timely."

The voters agree. Two thirds of the respondents in a *Tribune* poll give Ryan a thumbs-up. The people of Illinois from across the spectrum seem ready to take a second look at this whole business.

But for those citizens who are saying, "Thank God this couldn't happen in my state," the news is not all that reassuring. This parable unfolded in Chicago not because Illinois justice is more fallible but because it has an appellate system that's a cut above average, and because of a daily journalistic dogfight between the *Sun-Times* and the *Tribune* with the *Chicago Reader* nipping at their heels. Along with some remarkable college kids, the city's best journalists were given free rein to invest hundreds of hours in major investigations and with that kind of searchlight you can spot the cracks in almost anything—as Steve Mills and Ken Armstrong prove so conclusively when they turn their attention to Texas.

Their series on Lone Star justice exposes a system with all the faults of Illinois but with none of the saving graces. The appellate courts in Texas can't even agree on who's responsible for what. The state Court of Criminal Appeals only reviews questions of law—they leave the factual evidence and claims of innocence to the Board of Pardons and Paroles. But the Board of Pardons and Paroles says innocence is none of their business; they only advise the governor on questions of mercy. So claims of actual innocence in Texas don't even have a designated listener.[19]

The records of most other death penalty states contain the same kind of alarm signals that triggered the inquiry in Illinois but these states don't happen to have a bunch of journalism students and ace reporters hanging around with time on their hands. Of the 93 individuals who have now been rescued from death row, 20 of them came from Florida alone. Illinois followed with 13, Oklahoma and Texas had 7 apiece, Georgia 6, Arizona 5, and the balance were spread over 14 other states. Since 1976 only a dozen states have carried out executions without having to exonerate anyone. But it's hard to imagine that their slate would have remained clean if it had been subjected to the kind of journalistic scrutiny that saved Anthony Porter.

ROME—FEBRUARY 1, 2000

Despite its spectacular architecture, the Colosseum is undeniably a symbol of oppression. Here the lions ate the Christians, here the gladiators died at the whim of the emperor. So the Romans of today, who like most Europeans, oppose capital punishment, use the arena as a political signpost in their crusade against the death penalty. Whenever a prisoner anywhere in the world is spared execution, the Colosseum is illuminated with gold floodlights. Tonight the Colosseum is bathed in gold light to honor Governor George Ryan of Illinois.

> "WASHINGTON—A plan to ensure that every defendant facing a possible death sentence has a competent attorney ran into opposition Wednesday in Congress from death-penalty advocates who said it is unnecessary and would introduce an anti-capital punishment bias in the legal system."
> —*Los Angeles Times*, June 28, 2001

CHAPTER SIX

"After 20 years on the high court, I have to acknowledge that serious questions are being raised about whether the death penalty is being fairly administered in this country…If statistics are any indication, the system may well be allowing some innocent defendants to be executed."

—U.S. Supreme Court Justice Sandra Day
O'Connor, July 2001[1]

CHICAGO—JANUARY, 2000

Charles Hoffman got his start at the People's Law Office with Jeff Haas and Flint Taylor, but these days he's working for the State of Illinois. As an attorney for the Office of the State Appellate Defender, it's his job to handle the mandatory appeals that are now required for each Illinois death sentence.

In the wake of the astounding revelations breaking in the *Chicago Tribune* over the last few weeks, Hoffman is fielding a call from an out-of-town journalist. "How is it possible," the reporter asks, "for a prosecutor to cover up the confession of a man who is clearly guilty, and then continue to go after his original suspect as if nothing had happened?"

Hoffman says, "You have to consider who's the most convictable."

This sobering concept—"convictability"—snaps into focus the fundamental problem that underlies the entire U.S. criminal justice system: prosecutors are not rewarded for doing justice, they are rewarded for their conviction rate. Convictions, like notches on a six-gun, are the key to upward mobility and the rewards can be substantial. All new prosecutors can conjure a glimpse of themselves in the governor's mansion, and for some it's more than a glimpse. A significant percentage of the nation's judicial and political leadership rises from the ranks of former prosecutors—senators, congressmen, governors, supreme court justices—and the current mayors of Chicago, L.A. and New York.

Because the stakes are high, it's easy to see how otherwise honorable men and women find themselves tempted from time to time to bend the rules in order to maintain or improve their batting average. For one thing, the people they're going after have usually committed some horrible crime. And when you're looking at a scumbag with a five-page rap sheet who's charged with killing a cop—and you've got no solid evidence—it hardly seems unreasonable to accept the help of a jailhouse snitch, even though the snitch is a notorious liar who wants his sentence cut in half in return for testifying.

Then one day an alibi witness shows up who says the accused was with him the night of the murder. Well, clearly, this guy is lying. We already know who did it, and the last thing we need is to have this lying sonofabitch come to the attention of the defense attorneys. So the notes of this interview vanish into the night along with the witness.

But one day, looking over the original police reports, you realize there was another suspect—a much more likely one—that the cops never interviewed. What's more, the original police report contradicts several things the lead investigator told the grand jury.

Now this clearly calls for action. You have a legal and moral duty to inform the defense immediately. And of course you would if only the election weren't two weeks away.

This scenario, though it permeates our criminal justice system like sewer gas, does not suggest that prosecutors are any less moral than the rest of us. The vast majority of district attorneys are honest, hardworking public servants doing their level best to fight crime and keep the streets safe. The problem is that the checks and balances on their behavior are almost non-existent. In theory, the voters can always throw them out but that rarely happens to aggressive D.A.s no matter how many rules they break. Houston district attorney John Holmes was repeatedly castigated for running roughshod over the rights of defendants, and for two decades the Harris County voters couldn't get enough of him. The county commissioners responded to Holmes's critics by tripling his budget and doubling his staff. In his 21 years in office John Holmes sent over 200 people to death row—an all-time national record—and he was the most popular elected official in Houston's history.[2]

But over time, immunity from criticism can infuse public servants with a certain arrogance. As one of John Holmes's lieutenants recently said, "Convicting the guilty people is easy. The real challenge is in convicting someone who is innocent."[3]

The urgency to convict also creates a tolerance for short cuts. In a training video called "How to Pick a Jury," Philadelphia assistant D.A. Jack McMahon explains the facts of life to his new recruits: "Case law says that the object of selecting a jury is to get one that's competent, fair, and impartial," says McMahon. "Well, that's ridiculous. You're not trying to get that. If you go in there thinking you're some noble civil libertarian, you'll lose. You're there to win, and the only way to do that is to get jurors that are unfair and likely to convict."[4]

Unfortunately for McMahon, this tape fell into the wrong hands and his office was hit with a host of retrials. But McMahon himself suffered little more than a slap on the wrist. It's irrational to think that we can eliminate this kind of conviction insurance with an occasional harsh word.

Interestingly, federal prosecutors turn out to be no more ethical than their colleagues in the county courthouse. A 1998 investigation by the *Pittsburgh Post-Gazette* reviewed 1,500 allegations of official misconduct over the previous decade and their verdict was blood-curdling. "Hundreds of times during the past 10 years, federal agents and prosecutors have pursued justice by breaking the law. They lied, hid evidence, distorted facts, engaged in coverups, paid for perjury and set up innocent people in a relentless effort to win indictments, guilty pleas and convictions...

"Rarely were these federal officials punished for their misconduct. Rarely did they admit their conduct was wrong."[5]

LOS ANGELES—JANUARY, 2000

Mike Farrell is the tall blonde actor recognizable to millions of Americans as Capt. B.J. Hunnicutt from M*A*S*H, one of the longest-running shows on television. Unlike many of his contemporaries, Farrell skipped self-indulgence so he could trade on his celebrity in the service of good works. In fact, he is the archetypal Hollywood do-gooder, the bane of film industry conservatives like Ronald Reagan, and it was not surprising to find the two men on opposite sides of the fence during the Iran-Contra debacle. Farrell became an outspoken critic of the administration's policy in Central America.

Mike Farrell is a citizen-patriot who thinks the United States is the greatest country on earth and in serious need of improvement. Dedicated to abolition, he is president of Death Penalty Focus, a national reform group he helped put in motion, and over the last few years he has become one of the leading spokesmen in the campaign to end the death penalty.

Today he's at a North Hollywood lot shooting an episode of the TV series *Providence*, where he's the kindly veterinarian. In his trailer between takes, he's at his laptop forwarding the latest clippings from the *Chicago Tribune* series. Through the internet Farrell is in daily contact with hundreds of activists all over the country.

Critics would say Farrell is a limousine liberal whose experience of life has little relevance for the average Joe. What does he know about grief? How would he feel if some monster raped and killed his daughter?

"If somebody killed my wife or my daughter," says Farrell, "I'd want to strangle the sonofabitch with my bare hands. But what if the bastard I strangled with my bare hands wasn't the one who did it?"

At bottom, Farrell is opposed to the death penalty on moral grounds but those arguments don't have much traction these days. At the typical execution you find well-meaning citizens screaming at each other across the street, waving placards and shouting scripture—"An eye for an eye!" "Thou shalt not kill!"—and no minds are changed.

Farrell prefers to attack capital punishment on practical grounds and a lot of the information he and his associates have assembled over the last decade flies in the face of conventional wisdom. Deterrence for example. Most people assume the death penalty acts as a deterrent to murder. That's one of the obvious fundamental benefits. It turns out that's not the case. In fact, says Farrell, there is some evidence that executions may actually *increase* the murder rate.[6]

A study in Oklahoma compared murder rates before and after the state ended its 25-year moratorium on death in 1990. The author found no evidence of deterrence but he did find a significant *escalation* in the murder of strangers after executions were resumed.[7] And a California survey found

slight homicide increases in the months following the execution of Robert Alton Harris.[8] Some analysts believe that
these high-profile state-sponsored killings simply inspire bor-
derline psychotics. A geographical study comparing adjacent
border counties in pro- and anti-death penalty states found
there was a *higher* violent crime rate in the death penalty
counties.

In September, as if to underscore Farrell's point, the
New York Times publishes a survey showing that states without the death penalty have a better record on homicides.
Over the last twenty years, states with the death penalty had
homicide rates 50 to 100 percent higher than states without
the death penalty.[9] When the presidents of the leading criminological societies are asked if they think the death penalty
functions as a deterrent, over 90 percent say they know of no
evidence to support that claim.[10] Two-thirds of the police
chiefs and sheriffs who were surveyed came to the same conclusion.[11]

Deterrence is not the only fallacy on Mike Farrell's list.
A look at the cost of the death penalty is a revelation. Most
people naturally assume that executions save money. As one
Oklahoma City survivor says, "I don't want my tax dollars
paying for McVeigh's upkeep so he can sit around watching
TV." But it turns out the price of McVeigh's execution will
far and away exceed the cost of keeping him alive.

A California study shows that a capital trial in Los
Angeles County costs $1,900,000—three times as much as a
regular murder trial. The total bill for an execution there
runs around $2,100,000. Since life in prison averages about
$1,500,000, that would be a net saving of some $600,000 per
customer.[12] But the price of each execution is further driven
up by the fact that capital trials, though always expensive,

don't always result in conviction or death. When you factor in the misfires, the price skyrockets. *The Palm Beach Post* examined 44 executions in Florida that were carried out since 1976, and when you include all the capital convictions that were overturned on appeal and those cases where the jury wouldn't go for death, the cost of *completed* executions jumps to $24 million apiece. Overall, Florida spent about $1 billion more to kill these people than it would have cost to lock them up forever.[13]

Of course not everyone spends this kind of cash on capital trials. Most southern states don't like to waste money on defense attorneys and most rural counties simply don't have the resources. Unlike the $380,000 that Los Angeles spends on a capital public defender, there is a $1,000 limit in Mississippi. In Alabama a public defender can get $20 an hour—less in some Texas counties. The takers at these prices are going to be lawyers you wouldn't want representing you on a parking ticket. But even cut-rate death penalty efforts can break the bank. Tom Bridges, district attorney for San Patricio and Aransas counties on the Texas Gulf has a $290,000 annual budget for his whole operation. He could use that up on a single capital case. "And the next budget year," he says, "the commissioners would be looking at me like, 'You going to do that again?'"[15]

In Georgia, the *Savannah Morning News* reports that many small counties are being broken on the rack of the death penalty. Says Long County Administrator Richard Douglas, "If you're spending $300,000 for a case, that's $300,000 that could be used for buying road equipment, paying salaries, the fire and sheriff's departments...If you have two or three of these in a row, that can put you in a million dollar hole."[16]

On the other hand, you can't put a price on justice unless you're a county commissioner. The average citizen is willing to spend whatever it takes to see that a killer gets what he deserves, and without the hammer of retribution, civilization would quickly dissolve into anarchy. But as Mike Farrell points out, retribution is an issue quite separate from the question of death.

"If you ask people if they support the death penalty—yes or no—somewhere around seventy percent will say yes. But if you ask about alternatives like life without possibility of parole—or even better, life plus restitution, where the inmate works for the victim's family fund—the majority prefers that. That's a fact that has not fully permeated the public consciousness."

The latest numbers back up Farrell's argument. A January Gallup Poll shows that support for the death penalty has dropped to a 19-year low. The poll also reveals that nine out of ten people now believe that sometime in the past 20 years we have executed someone who's innocent.[17]

The State of Michigan avoided this problem altogether when they abandoned capital punishment in 1846. They now have over 2,500 inmates serving life without parole. State officials say these prisoners tend to cause fewer problems than the general prison population, they are generally quieter, not as insolent, are more likely to obey the rules and less likely to try to escape. Their motivation is simple: stay out of the hole. When they arrive they are locked up 23 hours a day and fed through a slot in the door. Only after a lengthy stretch of good behavior can they leave the hole to live in a regular cell, eat with other prisoners, or watch TV. One thing they can't do is get out. In Michigan, life without parole means you exit feet first.

Absolute certainty seems to be the key. One reason the

death penalty gained ground over the last three decades is because most Americans came to believe that the average killer would be out of prison in short order. As Illinois public defender Charles Hoffman admits, there was more than a little truth in that. "There were some really lenient laws," he says. "I mean, people could commit a murder and be back on the streets in ten years in Illinois. Nine years even. And I think the fact that the minimum sentences were so low caused people to think, 'The only way we can protect ourselves is if we sentence somebody to death because if we don't some bureaucrat is gonna let 'em out on parole!'"[18]

Most people don't know that there are other permanent solutions on the books. In the late 1970s when the death penalty was reinstated, other draconian alternatives were enacted at the same time. Illinois, for example, offers natural life without parole as an option. Natural life means until you're dead. Only the governor himself can touch that sentence.

This option has not been widely reported even where it's available and in some cases it has been intentionally suppressed. Death penalty proponents correctly see life without parole as a threat. When Texas tried to pass such a law in the early 1990s, the fiercest opponent was Harris County D.A. John Holmes. "I think it repeals the death penalty," he said. "I don't think you could get a verdict of death if the jury knows it can give a life sentence."[19]

Holmes, recently retired, almost single-handedly beat back life without parole because, as he put it, some people just don't deserve to live. His successor, Chuck Rosenthal, agrees. "We need to hold jurors to making the tough decision," he says. "I think jurors will shun away from making the hard decision when it is deserved if they have an out."[20]

Rosenthal, however, has nothing like the clout of his predecessor, so in the spring of 2001, with Holmes safely out of the way, the reformers try once again to give Texans the life-without-parole option that already exists in 46 other states. The bill fails in the House but this time it at least passes the Senate.

But even in states where the choice is available, fear of a non-death verdict often pushes prosecutors and judges to bizarre extremes in trying to keep the jury from hearing about those options. In *Weeks v. Angelone*,[21] the jury almost begs the judge for a clarification—Can they give the man life without parole instead of death?—and the judge merely refers them to his original ambiguous instruction. When they finally vote for death, the court reporter makes the remarkable note that all the jurors are crying.

This reticence to trust the jury with basic facts of life and death is only one stumbling block to reform, however. Another obstacle, says Hoffman, is the public perception of the prison as country club. During the tough-on-crime campaigns of the 1970s and 80s it was an article of faith among politicians that our prisons were "coddling criminals." Rehabilitation suddenly took a back seat to retribution, and prison officials, often against their better judgement, had to cut back on anything that wasn't associated with punishment—exercise equipment, libraries, job training, drug treatment, and education.

"Lots of people are shocked that the guy has a TV," says Hoffman. "'Why does he get to watch TV when his victim who's dead doesn't get to watch TV?' I don't think people understand that the TV is there just as much for the guards as the prisoner. If you lock people up without any kind of stimulus they're gonna go crazy. They're gonna be much more dangerous."

Politicians don't normally spend much time in prison, but we do catch one now and then and when they emerge from the slammer they are usually singing a different tune. Judge Sol Wachtler, former Chief Justice of the New York State Court of Appeals, has to do 11 months in federal prison for harassing his ex-girlfriend and the experience remodels his view of incarceration. Wachtler, although placed in a comparatively tame setting, is astounded by the routine brutality and constant fear. When another inmate stabs him in the back in the middle of the night, he is stitched up without anesthetic and thrown in the hole. The medics accuse him of stabbing himself to get attention.

As a judge, Wachtler had occasionally toured the New York State prison system and he was always impressed. Now he gets a chance to see the V.I.P. tour from the other side. "The guards are on their best behavior and troublesome inmates are either put in the hole or tucked away in some remote locale," he says. "The cabinets that house TV sets, always padlocked, are miraculously opened. And if we have the good fortune of having the visitors present during lunch, the meals are actually edible."

It occurs to Wachtler that he's part of a charade that will probably make everything worse. "The only thing accomplished by these tours is to create yet another group of propagandists who spread the word that life in prison is pretty good or—far more ominous for the future treatment of prisoners—that life in prison is too good."[22]

Wachtler is now a spokesman for prison reform and anyone who's ever followed in the former judge's footsteps and heard those steel doors clang understands this is no country club. "A maximum security prison is a pretty scary place," says Charles Hoffman. "And I don't know how many people think it would be fun to live in the bathroom for the rest of their lives."

TEXAS—JANUARY 19, 2001

Fourteen years ago Texas prosecutors offered Christopher Ochoa a deal. If he would confess to the rape and murder of Nancy DePriest, they would not press for the death penalty. Ochoa confessed, got life, and it was a good deal for everyone involved because it insured conviction, saved the state a lot of grief, and allowed Mr. Ochoa to keep breathing. It was a classic example of the importance of the death penalty as threat—the ultimate weapon in the prosecutor's arsenal. It has cracked many an otherwise intractable case.

So it is with a certain amount of chagrin that the State of Texas has to let Mr. Ochoa go today. Turns out he's not the guy. It seems the threat of death and the power of the prosecutor so overwhelmed Christopher Ochoa that he confessed to a murder he didn't commit.

On top of that, in the grand tradition of Lone Star judicial indifference, a detailed confession from the man who actually did it was completely ignored while Ochoa spent a dozen years in prison.[23]

Who finally cracked the case? Students, of course. This time from the University of Wisconsin. Successfully petitioning for a DNA test, they were able to establish once and for all that the murderer was not the man who was terrified into confessing. It was the man who confessed on his own.

OKLAHOMA CITY—1995

All his life Bud Welch has opposed the death penalty. Friends used to tell him that if anyone ever killed one of his family members, he would change. "What if Julie got raped and murdered?" But Welch always figured he'd stick to his guns. Until April 19.

Among the168 people whose lives vanish in the explosion at the Murrah Federal Building is Bud Welch's daughter, Julie. Welch is a Texaco dealer in downtown Oklahoma City. He was planning to have lunch with Julie at the Greek restaurant across the street on the day the bomb went off.

Welch's daughter was a wonder—a gorgeous young girl with a great heart. Just out of college, she was working as a translator for the Social Security Administration and dating a young Air Force officer. They were going to announce their engagement in two weeks. All gone in an instant.

In the weeks after the bombing Welch is consumed with visions of revenge and before long he's a wreck—drinking heavily, smoking three packs a day. More than anything else in the world, he wants to see Timothy McVeigh fried.

Patrick Reeder can match Bud Welch's hatred and raise it. Reeder lost his wife, Michelle, and he's an ex-Marine who knows how to kill people personally. "I wanted to stick my thumbs into Timothy McVeigh's windpipe and crush his larynx," he says. "You die very slowly that way. You basically suffocate. But before he was gone, I wanted to take out a knife and begin slicing off parts of his anatomy, starting with his most private parts first."[24]

An Oklahoma-born conservative Republican, Reeder has been a supporter of the death penalty all his life. He feels he owes it to Michelle to make sure McVeigh does not get out of this alive. Like Welch, he is drinking heavily and often goes days without food. As he sinks deeper into rage and revenge he finds himself screaming at people who cut him off in traffic. When somebody takes too long in the checkout line or the repairman shows up late, he's ready to punch them out.

It was for people like Patrick Reeder and Bud Welch that the Victims' Rights Movement came into being. Not so long ago, relatives and friends of murder victims were largely ignored by the criminal justice system. Prosecutors made deals without consulting the family members, and the survivors simply had to live with the consequences. When outraged relatives first appealed to lawmakers for some kind of relief they got nowhere. "They used to laugh at us," says activist Harriet Salarno.

In California, all that changed dramatically when Don Novey rode to the rescue. As a Sacramento lobbyist—and president of the state prison guards' union—Novey is one of the most powerful political players in the state. A top contributor to both parties, he and his organization are largely responsible for electing the state's last two governors. "When he speaks, they listen," says the *L.A. Times*.[25]

In the early 1990s Novey aligned his union with the Victims' Rights Movement and their combined moral and financial clout fundamentally altered the playing field. The personal experiences and heart-wrenching testimony from family members carries tremendous weight in a legislative hearing. Over the last decade the victims' lobby has been instrumental in toughening our treatment of criminals across the board. Now a force of remarkable power, they are reshaping the judiciary by ousting those judges and legislators who fail the "tough-on-crime" test.

Many of the Oklahoma City survivors and families find solace in the Victims' Rights Movement, but Bud Welch, still paralyzed with rage, isn't among them. One day he's sitting in a darkened room watching television and there is Bill McVeigh, the bomber's father. Welch's first reaction is to turn off the TV but for some reason he doesn't. There is something about the man, working in his garden. The reporter asks a question and Bill McVeigh glances up at the camera for a second or two. Bud Welch recognizes that look. That bottomless well of agony. "I knew right then that someday I had to go tell him that I truly cared how he felt."

Finally, Welch decides he has to go back to the scene. On a cold January afternoon eight months after the bombing, he heads downtown and stands across the street watching the hundreds of people circling the fence around the site. It begins to dawn on him that he's not going to feel any different after McVeigh is dead. Julie is gone. That's the unbearable truth. All he's got is rage and hatred. Somehow that hardly seems like a fitting memorial to his daughter.

As he looks across the empty void where the building used to stand, it occurs to him that in a strange way he's being sucked along by McVeigh's logic. It was McVeigh's hatred and revenge over the FBI raid in Waco that killed Julie.

Three months later Patrick Reeder sees a newspaper article about Bud Welch and he can't believe his eyes. Here's a guy who's daughter was just blown up and he's saying he doesn't want McVeigh executed.

"What a fool," says Reeder.

By the summer of 1996 Reeder has lost so much weight that his family has to check him into a hospital. The therapist says he's trying to kill himself.

But while Reeder is moved by the pain that many other survivors and family members are feeling, he finds himself increasingly disturbed by the hint of blood lust in their public statements. Everybody's saying it's about justice, not vengeance, but he knows better. It's about vengeance. He feels that urge himself.

Bud Welch, on the other hand, has become a full-time crusader against the death penalty. When Reeder catches him on television from time to time, Welch no longer seems as distraught. Or as foolish as Reeder once thought. "Here's a man who had suffered at least as much as I had," says Reeder.

"Everyone says losing a child is the worst thing that can happen to you. Yet he's still able to find it in his heart to ask for mercy for McVeigh."

Welch, in fact, has discovered a whole new group of fellow sufferers whose take on the problem is quite different from the rest of the Victims' Rights Movement. The organization is called Murder Victims' Families for Reconciliation. Headed by former New Hampshire State Representative Renny Cushing, MVFR is an advocacy group working for abolition of the death penalty. Cushing, whose father was killed by an off-duty cop in 1988, thinks the death penalty debate often turns on purely political considerations. "Some individuals wrestle with it," he says. "They actually believe it's an appropriate policy to take—based on faulty premises, I believe—but they have at least tried to think about the issue. Some people support it just out of rank political opportunism, sheer demagoguery. They feel it's an issue they can ride to power on."

But there is also an element of self preservation. "It's awfully difficult to cast a vote of conscience in opposition to the wishes of the majority of your constituents," says Cushing. When he was in the New Hampshire House, a fellow legislator told him he was lucky because his father's murder gave him the political cover to oppose the death penalty.

Cushing calls that "seeing the bright side."

OKLAHOMA CITY—2000

In the battle over capital punishment, the playing field between the two victims' rights movements is still tilted in favor of the pro-death penalty groups because they are the natural allies of pro-death penalty legislators and prosecutors. When Florida MVFR member Suezann Bosler tries to testify before the legislature in Tallahassee, she is roundly ignored by the lawmakers. The pro-death penalty families, on the other hand, are guests of Governor Jeb Bush.[26] In some jurisdictions it's worse. Desire for revenge is a prerequisite for access to therapy over grief. Prosecutors make it clear that assistance and counseling will only be available if you support the death penalty.

Bud Welch has become a major spokesman for the abolition movement. And as he travels the country speaking out against capital punishment, his efforts do not go unnoticed back home. There is criticism aplenty among the other survivors. But here and there various individuals are starting to voice their own reservations about McVeigh's execution—including Patrick Reeder.

"There was no moment of revelation for me," says Reeder. "It was just a slow, gradual process. At some point, I just realized something was really wrong here, and I started to think about who I was and what I really valued in my life." He has finally given up his fantasy of crushing McVeigh's larynx—though he makes no promises about what he would do if they were locked in a room together.

Reeder's heart goes out to the others, those who are still determined to see McVeigh get the needle. "I know a lot of families who are still in deep pain over this," he says. "I pray McVeigh's death helps them. I really do." But as for Patrick Reeder, he's now in Bud Welch's camp.

TERRE HAUTE, INDIANA—MAY, 2001

Since the United States restored the death penalty 25 years ago, 60 other countries have chosen to abolish it. We are now in the rarified company of Saudi Arabia and Iraq. With the rest of the world heading in the opposite direction, America's acceleration of capital punishment has astounded our allies. President Clinton's ambassador to France found it was the first question asked wherever he spoke: How could the world's champion of human rights be so at odds with the sweep of history?[27]

Nonetheless, in spite appeals for clemency from every corner of the planet and resounding condemnation throughout Europe, the U.S. Justice Department is in the middle of a military countdown to the execution of Timothy McVeigh.

Then, with less than a week remaining, Attorney General John Ashcroft rocks the nation with word that the FBI has uncovered 3,000 pages of evidence that should have been turned over to McVeigh's lawyers. The bureau's defenders try to pass it off as a clerical error but the implications are stupefying. The *New York Post* sums it up: "If ever there were a case where it was important for the government to play by the rules, it was this one," says conservative columnist Rod Dreher. "And still they fumbled." A longtime supporter of the death penalty, Dreher has changed his mind. "After the McVeigh debacle, who can trust our government to administer capital punishment? ...what of the anonymous cases where the defendant's guilt is less obvious?"[28]

Despite this finish-line speed bump, the pressure for McVeigh's execution is inexorable. There is no doubt about his guilt. He confessed. What's more he's cooperating. He wants this over with.

A few minutes before seven on the morning of June 11, Timothy McVeigh hops onto the fatal gurney and helps the guards as they strap him down. Having cast himself in the role of warrior, he remains defiant to the end, acknowledging each witness with a nod, then fixing his gaze on the overhead camera.

Six hundred miles west, a tent full of Oklahoma City survivors and family members wait on folding chairs for the poison to flow. Attorney General Ashcroft has arranged for a closed-circuit broadcast to accommodate the 232 witnesses who could not fit in the tiny chamber in Terre Haute.

The screen flickers and there is the focus of their hatred, the man who has brought them more agony than they knew existed.

McVeigh has always been a mystery to them, but those hoping for a last-second glimpse into his soul find only disappointment. He has no intention of revealing himself now. He stares at the camera unbowed.

And then he is gone.

For some of the witnesses there is a creeping sensation that he got off easy. Jay Sawyer, whose mother fell four stories to her death, recalls that she was terrified of heights. He wanted McVeigh to experience some of that terror. Instead he just went to sleep.

"I thought I would feel something more satisfying," he says. "But I don't."[29]

VIRGINIA—JUNE, 2001

The ghastly parade now seems endless. By mid-summer, nearly a hundred people nationwide have walked away from death row under their own power. Supporters of capital punishment say this shows the system works. They remind us that no one has come up with legal proof that we have executed an innocent person.

Technically this is correct. There has never been a courtroom demonstration that the state has taken an innocent life. But that has less to do with innocence than the fact that the case is closed when your client is executed. Nobody has time to save a dead man. When Houston attorney Dick Burr lost Gary Graham after nine years of continuous combat, he had to jump on the next case almost immediately.

Attempts have been made, however, to document those instances where the stench is overwhelming. One major effort, *In Spite of Innocence,* by Michael Radelet, Hugo Bedau and Constance Putnam, documents 23 cases where the authors are convinced that an innocent person was executed.[30] Of course there's no way these charges can be adjudicated since there is no earthly court to take them to.

But in the spring of 2001 the State of Virginia finally has an opportunity to settle the argument, at least in one high profile case. Ten years ago death row inmate Roger Coleman claimed to be innocent right to his last gasp, but because his appeal was three days late—his lawyer forgot—the federal court refused to hear his claim and he was executed.[31] It seems, however, that a sample of the semen from the crime scene still exists in a lab in California, and while the DNA test wasn't definitive at the time of trial, the new tests are much more sensitive. So in late 2000 the *Boston Globe* and several other organizations petition the Virginia courts seeking a test of the sample to settle Coleman's guilt or innocence once and for all.

Virginia Circuit Judge Keary Williams turns them down. He says there would be "no benefit" to society.

If by "society" the judge is referring to himself and his colleagues, that is certainly true. Had the DNA test proved Coleman innocent, then the judicial system Judge Williams represents would be guilty of murder. How do you deal with that?

In an attempt to slam the door on this potential mortification once and for all, Virginia law enforcement officials demand the return of the semen sample. Dr. Robert Blake, the forensic scientist whose California lab is storing the sample, flatly refuses. While he may not be able to perform the test without a court order, he's not going to let go of the goods in the meantime, no matter what. "They want to seize this evidence and flush it," he says. "I'm not going to go along with that."[32] As of this writing the stalemate continues.

NEW ORLEANS—JULY, 2001

The Fifth Circuit Court of Appeals is debating whether or not a lawyer must be actually awake during a death penalty trial in order to adequately represent his client. The point at issue is whether he slept through anything really important. All sides agree he was awake for some of the trial, but they're equally certain he was out cold from time to time despite his client's attempt to wake him up.

When the case was originally appealed to a three-judge panel of the Fifth Circuit, they looked over the record and decided 2-to-1 that counsel probably hadn't slept through anything important. In fact the record didn't have all that much in it. There were few objections, so things must have gone pretty smoothly. The court advised Texas to proceed with the execution.

But people unschooled in the law began to ask if the reason for such a sparse trial record might not be the fact that the defendant's lawyer was, for all practical purposes, out of the room. In the public wildfire that followed, the Fifth Circuit agreed to rehear the arguments before the full 14-judge panel.

Now the argument is in full sway and Judge Rhesa Barksdale, one of the two jurists who denied the appeal the first time around, is still adamant. He acknowledges that the trial record reflects periods of inactivity, but that doesn't prove that the lawyer was sleeping. He says it's possible that he merely appeared to be asleep as part of his "trial strategy." Siding with Judge Barksdale, as she did on the original panel, is Judge Edith Jones, said to be on President Bush's short list for the Supreme Court. Where is the proof, she asks. How do we know the lawyer would have done any better if he'd been awake?

But for Judge Fortunato Benavides, the issue isn't all that complicated: "Unconscious counsel equates to no counsel at all." His argument carries the day 9-to-5 and the court orders a new trial for Calvin Burdine.[33]

Should the case make it to the Supreme Court, which it probably will, those nine good men and women will have to try once again to readjust the death penalty machinery they set in motion with *Gregg v. Georgia* in 1976.

OKLAHOMA CITY—AUGUST, 2001

Governor Frank Keating of Oklahoma is a devout Catholic but he doesn't go along with the idea of Papal infallibility. "The Pope is wrong on this issue," he says. "I believe in the death penalty." When he ran for office he swore he would never grant clemency to anyone on death row. In Oklahoma, as in Texas, that's not only good politics, it's common sense. But Keating, like his fellow governor George Ryan of Illinois, had not figured on the astounding revelations available in a few molecules of DNA.

When Malcolm Rent Johnson was executed in January 2000 for rape and murder, his death was surrounded by controversy over the trial testimony of Oklahoma City forensic chemist Joyce Gilchrist. A 21-year veteran of the police department crime lab, Gilchrist testified that semen consistent with Johnson's blood type was found in the victim's bedroom. But there were rumors already circulating in the back stairs at city hall that Ms. Gilchrist might have been faking evidence, and now these rumors are gaining credibility.

This sends a jolt through the building because Gilchrist has testified in over 1400 criminal trials. The potential liability for the city, not to mention the cost of hundreds of retrials, is like a bucket of water in the face. It gets everybody's attention. The authorities begin gingerly turning over a rock or two and soon the investigation blossoms into a review of Gilchrist's entire case file. In May of 2001 the state has to release a man who spent 15 years in prison for rape and murder based on Gilchrist's word. She said the hair was his. His DNA just proved otherwise. Then a federal appeals court overturns a death sentence because of problems with Gilchrist's testimony.

In July comes even more unsettling news. When Gilchrist testified in the case of Malcolm Rent Johnson a dozen years ago she said she found semen consistent with his blood type on the slides in evidence. An independent lab has just confirmed the worst. There isn't any semen on the slides she used to determine the match. Johnson, unfortunately, will not benefit from this discovery. He was executed 18 months ago.

When the FBI is called in to take a look, their verdict is even more chilling. The bureau's experts say Gilchrist is not only guilty of shoddy work, but she testified "beyond the acceptable limits of forensic science." In other words, she didn't know what she was talking about.

Already on administrative leave, Gilchrist is fired from her $60,000 job in September as the city battens the hatches for the coming storm. The implications are staggering. In addition to Malcolm Johnson, there are ten other cases where Gilchrist's testimony helped send the defendants to the death chamber. In at least five of these cases the FBI says Gilchrist's work was indefensible.[34]

U.S. SUPREME COURT—JUNE 20, 2002

Convicted murderer John Paul Penry draws like a child. He thinks like a child. With an I.Q. of around 59, he's essentially a seven-year-old inside a grown man's body. The State of Texas has been trying to execute him for two decades, so far unsuccessfully. He's already been snatched from the jaws of death twice by the Supreme Court, both times with minutes to spare. But today's ruling seems to put the capstone on any further attempt to kill him.

Reversing their 1989 decision, the high court now finds that executing the mentally retarded is cruel and unusual punishment prohibited by the constitution. When they last considered this question, only two of the 38 death-penalty states prohibited executing the retarded. Now it's 18 states and the court is swayed by this shift in public opinion, ruling 6-to-3 that the mentally child-like should not be put to death.

The reaction in the Lone Star state is swift and certain. Two weeks later, prosecutors in Conroe, Texas, explain to the jury that in order to execute John Paul Penry, they will have to find that he is no longer mentally retarded. The jurors quickly determine that his intellect is sufficient for a lethal injection, and John Paul Penry is now back on death row for the fourth time.

DETROIT—AUGUST 26, 2002

Seventeen years ago Wayne County Circuit Judge Leonard Townsend looked down from the bench at convicted rapist Eddie Lloyd and lamented the fact that he couldn't sentence him to death. In his confession, Lloyd had described every detail of the brutal rape and murder of a Detroit teenager, including the green bottle left in her rectum. But Judge Townsend's hands were tied. The State of Michigan doesn't allow the death penalty.

And that in the long run turned out to be fortunate indeed for Judge Townsend, because today he looks down from the bench and announces that there has been a terrible mistake. Eddie Lloyd is free to go. DNA evidence, uncovered by the indomitable Barry Scheck after a seven-year crusade, proves conclusively that the killer was someone else.

At the time of his arrest, Eddie Lloyd was in a mental institution diagnosed as a paranoid schizophrenic. When he called the police to ask about the case, they assumed he was the killer and that was the end of the investigation. According to Lloyd, detective Thomas De Galan convinced him that if he signed the confession it would help smoke out the real killer. The information in the confession was apparently fed to him line by line. According to Lloyd, the detective asked questions like, "What kind of jeans was she wearing?"

"I said, 'I don't know.' He said, 'What kind do you think?' I said, 'Jordache.' He said, 'No, Gloria Vanderbilt.'" Lloyd says the detective then guided him through a sketch of the crime scene.

Attorney Barry Scheck thinks the prime mover for this travesty was political expedience. The brutal murder was a "heater case" and months had passed with no arrest. "This cop had to know," says Scheck, "he was feeding...a guy with a mental disorder, in a mental instituton, facts in order to clear a major homicide so everybody could look good."

Eddie Lloyd is the 103rd U.S. prisoner to hear the gates unlock since the Innocence Project began using DNA as a lifesaver. But his release highlights an alarming detail contained within that number. According to Scheck, 20 percent of these innocent souls were somehow beguiled, tricked, or tortured into signing false confessions.

BOSTON—SEPTEMBER 16, 2002

"There was some skepticism that we would ever bring to justice one of our own," says U.S. Attorney Michael Sullivan, "but this day had to come." Sullivan is at the federal court house in Boston for the sentencing of FBI agent John J. Connolly Jr., a top dog in the Boston office who turned out to be a double agent. Mr. Connolly, who always had amazing inside info on the mob, apparently got it by giving the mob inside info on the Justice Department.

Today he will receive the maximum, 10 years, but his shame is nothing alongside that of the people he worked for. The rap sheet on his employers is so horrifying that it strains credibility. Not only were individual agents in bed with the mob, but key agents up to and including J. Edgar Hoover himself were involved in the coverup. Most ominous is the chilling evidence that the Boston FBI office, with the full knowledge of Washington, allowed two innocent men to be sentenced to life in prison—and two others to death row—in order to keep one of their informants on the streets.

In early 1965, Boston agents had an illegal bug planted in the headquarters of the Patriarca Mafia family when they overheard a hit being planned by their own informant. Joseph "The Animal" Barboza was a notorious hit man who had been recruited with the approval of Director J. Edgar Hoover.

Hoover, at that moment, was under tremendous pressure to do something about the Mafia. Throughout the 1950s, he had focused the agency on rooting out Communists, and he completely dismissed the Mafia as a screenwriter's fantasy. But when photos of a gangland conclave in upstate New York made the center spread of *LIFE* Magazine, Hoover was on the griddle. To rescue the agency from an unaccustomed torrent of media abuse, he would have to produce instant results on totally unfamiliar terrain. The obvious solution was to make a deal with the Devil. Up in Boston, Joseph Barboza was signed on even though Hoover knew he was a professional killer who would kill again.

And he did. The hit he planned was successful but there was a lot of gunplay and Barboza was quickly nabbed by the Boston police. He volunteered to cooperate in return for a light sentence. He then named four innocent men he didn't particularly like and pinned the whole thing on them.

The FBI was aware of all this but Headquarters decided that Barboza was such a valuable informant that they'd have to go along with his story. These four innocent chaps would just have to donate their lives to the greater good.

The four were convicted on the strength of Barboza's testimony and two of them got life. Two were sentenced to death. And as they were dragged away, the top men at the nation's premier law enforcement agency kept their mouths shut.

There were a couple of winners in this sordid affair. Director Hoover and the agency got some excellent press when the Patriarca crime family was finally crushed. And the Patriarca's underworld competitors did okay, too. What no one knew at the time was that the FBI agents had achieved their stunning success against Patriarca by going into business with the Winter Hill mob. Once Patriarca was wiped out, the Winter Hill mob then had a free hand to take over the local drug trade and to blow people away now and then while the FBI looked the other way.

Rep. Dan Burton of Indiana is a law-and-order Republican who's always been a fan of the FBI. But when his committee finally got a look at the Boston transcripts, the congressman's first thought was to call for removing J. Edgar Hoover's name from the headquarters building in Washington.

The four fall guys fought unsuccessfully for 33 years to

get out of prison until the frayed edges of the coverup finally came apart. By then it was too late for two of the victims. Henry Tameleo and Louis Greco died in prison. Peter Limone, sentenced to death in the electric chair, was saved from a state murder in 1974 when Massachusetts outlawed the death penalty. He and Joseph Salvati, along with other victims of the Boston FBI-mob partnership, are suing the agency for half-a-billion dollars.

But no cash settlement, however staggering, can obscure the enormity of this debacle. In its simplest terms, key officials at the nation's top law enforcement agency sent two innocent men to death row as a matter of political convenience. The agency's reputation was at stake.

If this kind of moral cancer can be festering at the highest levels of the FBI—our most trusted crime-fighting institution—it is sobering to speculate on what might be happening around the country at the hands of less professional lawmen.

CHICAGO—JANUARY 11, 2003

In the 36 months since Governor George Ryan put a lid on executions in Illinois, he has been besieged by both camps. A hero to the abolition movement, he gets a standing ovation wherever he speaks, while prosecutors and lawmen deride him as a party hack who's trying to deflect attention from a corruption scandal.

Back in January 2000, right after he called for the moratorium, the governor named a blue ribbon panel to analyze the death penalty machinery and see if it could be fixed. Two years later the commission turns in a list of 85 repairs they feel are essential for the system to work—from tougher standards for lawyers to videotaping the whole interrogation instead of just the confession; from eliminating orchestrated line-ups to banning death for those convicted solely on the word of a single witness or a jailhouse snitch.

All of this, of course, is a non-starter down in Springfield. As State Senator Kirk Dillard says, "Legislators like to get tougher and tougher on crime. We ratchet it up, not down." He and his fellow lawmakers are also hearing from their colleagues in law enforcement. They are going through the roof. As Cook County State's Attorney Mike Devine says, "We are responsible to the people we serve and he has made it abundantly clear that he is not."

In the end, the death penalty supporters overwhelm the reformers. Throughout the 2002 session the legislators refuse to touch a single major reform. But it is a Pyrrhic victory. The governor, stung by the rebuke, begins talking about total amnesty for everybody on death row.

When he announces that he is going to review every single capital case, Devine and the others come back with a vengeance. They demand public hearings where they are able to present the relatives and survivors. The heart-wrenching testimony from these tormented families, still waiting for justice, almost stops Ryan in his tracks.

But the governor is equally impressed with the fact that his tormentors have never addressed the root problem that set this whole thing in motion: 13 exonerations, 12 executions. That's worse than 50-50. Are these guys saying that's acceptable?

And in their determination to vilify him, Divine and his colleagues seem to have forgotten a pivotal fact. At the moment, George Ryan is a man without a leash. Because of the corruption scandal, he's already announced he's not running again. And in Illinois, on the issue of clemency, the governor's word is absolute.

With three days remaining in his term, he steps to the

podium at Northwestern University Law School and the abolitionist crowd is on its feet. Word has leaked about the decision.

Now this pharmacist from Kankakee, a minor Republican functionary who planned to leave no permanent tracks on the public record, delivers a simple speech that will define the death penalty debate from this point forward. After a sledgehammer critique of the state's capital punishment system, he wipes the slate.

"Because our three year study has found only more questions about the fairness of the sentencing; because of the spectacular failure to reform the system...because the Illinois death penalty system is arbitrary and capricious... I no longer shall tinker with the machinery of death. I cannot say it more eloquently than Justice Blackmun.

"The legislature couldn't reform it. Lawmakers won't repeal it. But I will not stand for it. I must act.

"Our capital system is haunted by the demon of error, error in determining guilt, and error in determining who among the guilty deserves to die. Because of all of these reasons, today I am commuting the sentences of all death row inmates."

With that, one hundred sixty-four capital sentences are commuted to life without parole. Four others get a full pardon. Three of them walk out the door. They were on death row because of confessions extracted at the hands of Detective Jon Burge in the "House of Screams."

LOS ANGELES—FEBRUARY, 2003

This investigation was intended as an engineering analysis of capital punishment as a system. Leaving the legalities and moral arguments aside, does it work? The results are not promising.

Capital punishment does not function as a deterrent. The evidence here is so one-sided that most academic death penalty advocates have dropped this argument altogether.[35]

Nor does it save money. Again, the evidence is unequivocal.[36]

It does function as a powerful threat in the hands of an unprincipled prosecutor who needs a confession, but beating the suspect senseless with a telephone book will usually accomplish the same thing.

It does eliminate any threat that the killer will be released to kill again, but as Michigan and several other states attest, so does life without parole.

There are a couple of arguments, however, that the capital punishment supporters carry away hands-down. When it comes to retribution, killing the killer is perfectly symmetrical. And back in the old days, it usually worked. As Pecos Judge Roy Bean said to the ranchers who caught a cattle rustler red-handed, "What did you bring him here fer? Take him away and string him up."

But instantaneous retribution only functions on the frontier. Under the present system, even the most optimistic capital punishment advocates admit that anything less than five years from conviction to execution is probably impossible.

Which leads us to the ultimate argument in favor of death: closure. That is certainly what many if not most of the relatives and families watching Timothy McVeigh's last breath were seeking, and hopefully they found it.

But when the dust settles, most survivors say "closure" is a myth. And the execution itself is often a bitter disappointment. The day finally arrives after years of interminable courtroom games and they find the press focused entirely on the killer. Their children or wives or husbands are mere bit players in the drama if they are mentioned at all. Then the curtain is pulled aside for a moment and the object of their hatred goes to sleep. A frequent complaint is that the sonofabitch didn't suffer enough. At this point drawing and quartering begins to make sense.

In the case of the Nicarico family of DuPage County, the prosecutors promised closure and instead gave them six separate trials and an opportunity to re-live every grisly detail of their daughter's death over and over and over again. But suppose the DuPage prosecutors had been rewarded for a low crime rate rather than a high conviction rate. And suppose they had not been tempted by the publicity of a notorious capital trial. If, say, they had asked for life instead of death, there would have been no endless wait for justice. The sentence could have begun the minute Rolando Cruz was convicted back in 1985.

Ironically, this might have turned out worse for Cruz and better for the prosecution. Without the death penalty hanging over him, Cruz's innocence would probably never have been investigated.

In the last analysis, the families of the victims seem to hold the key. Their voices carry considerable weight, and with good reason. But they are not united in their demand for blood.

Sitting in the office of the Illinois Appellate Defender west of the Chicago Loop, Charles Hoffman tries to frame the issue in terms of those most affected. "The family of the victim wants to feel that their slain family member is as valuable as any other victim," he says. "It's somehow an insult, or lessening the memory, if the killer of their loved one isn't given the maximum. And so the very existence of the death penalty causes people to clamor for the death penalty." But if there were no capital punishment, he says, most people would probably be satisfied with a sentence of life without parole since that would be the absolute maximum available. It's an interesting idea, and in fact it's already working in Michigan and elsewhere.

The U.S.A. may be the greatest country on earth, as we are fond of saying, and looking at criminal justice around the world it would be easy to conclude that our setup is among the best. But we could use a little humility on all counts. Our legal system is operated by folks like us, ordinary humans capable of greatness and stupidity. On that latter point the record is abundantly clear. As Richard Nixon used to say, "Mistakes were made."

This doesn't mean we can't have the death penalty. We can continue to tinker with it, make it more fair to poor people and minorities, insist on some kind of decent counsel, force the prosecutors to come clean, and we will still get it wrong because humans and mistakes go together like coffee and donuts.

If we insist on capital punishment, we must not try to deny the bargain we are striking. From time to time we will be killing an innocent citizen.

Just hope it isn't you.

> *"It's a penalty we reserve for people who can't afford the finest lawyers."*
> —Former Illinois Supreme Court Justice
> Seymour Simon[37]

Notes

CHAPTER ONE

1   *Miranda v. State of Arizona*, 384 U.S. 436 (1966).

2   Time estimates from Ms. Skillern's trial testimony, Volume XV, at 331, 389.

3   *Houston Chronicle*, June 18, 2000, "A Question of Justice."

4   Offense Report, p.10-11.

5   Offense Report, p.35: "After the showup Mrs. Skillern was taken into the hall by Ellis and stated that the person she saw shoot the comp was the man in the #3 position (Graham). She stated that she was positive this was the man. Mrs. Skillern was very nervous and prior to the showup had indicated that she did not wish the attorneys to be present when she talked to Ellis concerning a possible identification. The attorneys were made aware of this request and stood several feet away while Ellis talked to Skillern in the hall."

6   Offense Report, p.35; *The Wall Street Journal*, July 19, 2000, Letters, "The Gary Graham Defense," Jack Zimmerman. Officer quoted.

7   *New York Times*, "Texas Lawyer's Death Row Record a Concern.", June 11, 2000

8   *New York Times*, "Texas Lawyer's Death Row Record a Concern.", June 11, 2000

9   Trial Transcript, Vol. XVI, page 440.

10 Proposed Finding of Fact and Conclusions of Law and Order, ¶ 32-33, April 26, 1993, *Ex parte Gary Graham*, No. 335378-B, 182nd District Court of Harris County.

11 Elizabeth Loftus, Ph.D., *Eyewitness Testimony*, Harvard University Press, Cambridge, 1996.

12 Offense Report, p17

13 *Chicago Tribune*, "Death Row Justice Derailed," Ken Armstrong and Steve Mills, Nov. 14-18, 1999.

14 *New York Times*, "Capital Errors", June 23, 2000

15 Michael Radelet, Hugo Bedau, Constance Putnam, *In Spite of Innocence*, Northwestern University Press, Boston, 1992, p66-72; *Amarillo Globe-News*, "Report Criticizes Texas Executions.", June 12, 2000

16 *The Dallas Morning News* reported in May, 2000 that hair analysis expert Charles Linch had been committed to a psychiatric ward for drinking and depression in 1994. Although considered a danger to himself and others, he was released to testify against Kenneth McDuff. McDuff was executed in 1998.

17 *Chicago Tribune*, "Flawed Trials Lead to Death Chamber," June 11, 2000.

18 "Nearly one in three young African American men (ages 21 to 29) in Texas is under some form of criminal justice control—either prison, jail or on parole or probation." *Austin American-Statesman*, "The Color of Texas Justice," Sept. 5, 2000

19 Associated Press, June 23, 2000, "Europe Outraged Over U.S. Execution," by Colleen Barry.

20 Dick Burr, interview, Houston, June 20, 2000.

21 *New York Times*, "In Death Row Dispute, a Witness Stands Firm.", June 16, 2000

22 *New York Times*, June 16, 2000, "In Death Row Dispute, a Witness Stands Firm." "According to the trial transcript, Ms Skillern testified that she saw Mr. Graham 'off and on about 60 seconds, maybe a little longer.' She told the jury that she had seen the side of his face, and that she had then blown her horn, at which point she looked directly at his face for 'a split second.' Today she repeated roughly the same story, saying that she had seen the killer's face from different angles three or four times over 90 seconds. Looking through her windshield, she said, she looked directly into his face when he walked in front of her headlights, about a car distance away."

23 *New York Times*, June 18, 2000, "I Was Certain, but I Was Wrong" by Jennifer Thompson.

24 Three affidavits, names redacted, sworn and signed before Gene H. Boyd, Notary for the State of Texas, June 15, 2000; copies provided by Zimmerman and Burr.

25 *New York Times*, June 21, 2000, "2 Men, Fates Linked: Nation Watches as Bush Prepares To Act in the Case of Gary Graham."

26 *New York Times*, June 21, 2000, "2 Men, Fates Linked: Nation Watches as Bush Prepares To Act in the Case of Gary Graham."

27 *New York Times*, June 21, 2000, "Pending Execution in Texas Spotlights a Powerful Board."

28 Offense Report, p16.

29 *Houston Chronicle*, June 23, 2000, "Graham Executed After Struggle."

30 Dick Burr, interview , offices of Burr & Welch, Houston, June 23, 2000.

31 *Houston Chronicle*, June 23, 2000, "Graham Executed After Struggle."

32 *Houston Chronicle*, June 23, 2000, "Graham Executed After Struggle."

33 *Herrera v. Collins*, 506 U.S. 390, 428 (1993) (Scalia, J., Concurring).

CHAPTER TWO

1   Death Penalty Information Center "History of the Death Penalty."

2   Death Penalty Information Center "History of the Death Penalty."

3   Cesare Beccaria, *An Essay on Crimes and Punishments*, E.D. Ingraham, trans. Philadelphia, H. Nicklin, 1819.

4   Death Penalty Information Center "History of the Death Penalty."

5   *New York Times*, "12 Years In Death Row," Feb 19, 1960.

6   *New York Times*, "Chessman Dies: Denies His Guilt," May 3, 1960.

7   Anthony Amsterdam, interview, April 13, 2001.

8   *New York Times*, "Court to Rule on Death Penalty," June 29, 1971.

9   *New York Times*, February 19, 1972, p.1.

10 Jose M. Ferrer III, *World* Magazine, "The Plot to Kill Captial Punishment, November 7, 1972.

11 Anthony Amsterdam, interview, April 13, 2001.

12 Dept. of Justice, Bureau of Justice Statistics, Source Book of Criminal Justice Statistics,1999 Gallup Poll: "Are you in favor of the death penalty for a person convicted of murder?'

13 Anthony Amsterdam, interview, April 13, 2001.

14 *The Law and Politics Book Review*, C. Neal Tate, ed., ISSN 1062-7421 Univ. of North Texas, 1996.

15 Sharlitt, Joe H., *Fatal Error: The Miscarriage of Justice that Sealed the Rosenberg's*

Fate. Quoted in Bedau *Death Penalty in America* 242.

16 *Wainwright v. Sykes*.

17 Millard Farmer, Joe Nursey, Kimellen Tunkle, *Death Row, U.S.A.*

18 Millard Farmer, Joe Nursey, Kimellen Tunkle, *Death Row, U.S.A.*

19 The Baldus Study, as presented to the Supreme Court, is published in David C. Baldus et al, "Monitoring and Evaluating Contemporary Death Sentencing Systems: Lessons from Georgia," 18 *U.C. Davis Law Rev.* 1375 (1985).

20 Professor Dennis D. Dorin, Univ. of North Carolina, interview, May 16, 2001.

21 *McCleskey v. Kemp*, 481 US 279.

22 Dennis D. Dorin, "Far Right of the Mainstream: Racism, Rights, and Remedies From the Perspective of Justice Antonin Scalia's *McCleskey* Memorandum," *Mercer Law Review*, 45, 3 (Spring 1995) 1035-1088

23 *Memorandum to the Conference from Justice Antonin Scalia* in No. 84-6811— *McCleskey v. Kemp* of Jan. 6, 1987. *McCleskey v. Kemp* File, THURGOOD MARSHALL PAPERS, The Library of Congress: "I disagree with the argument that the inferences that can be drawn from the Baldus study are weakened by the fact that each jury and each trial is unique, or by the large number of variables at issue. And I do not share the view, implicit in [Justice Powell's draft opinion], that an effect of racial factors upon sentencing, if it could be shown by sufficiently strong statistical evidence, would require reversal... Since it is my view that the unconscious operation of irrational sympathies and antipathies, including racial, upon jury decisions and (hence) prosecutorial [ones], is real, acknowledged by the [cases] of this court and ineradicable, I cannot honestly say that all I need is more proof."

24 *Plessy v. Ferguson*, 163 U.S. 537, 552

25 *McCleskey v. Kemp*, 481 US 279, 314-15.

26 *McCleskey v. Kemp*, 481 US 279, 339.

27 *McCleskey v. Kemp*, 481 US 279, 321.

28 *McCleskey v. Kemp*, 481 US 279, 344.

29 *Woodward v. Hutchins*, 464 US 377 (Jan 13, 1984).

30 Alex Kozinski, "Tinkering With Death," *The New Yorker*, Feb 10, 1997, p.50.

31 Hugo Bedau ed., *Death Penalty in America*, Oxford Univ. Press, NY, 1997, p.241.

32 Radelet, Bedau, Putnam, *In Spite of Innocence*, xii.

33 *Callins v. Collins*, 114 S. Ct. 1127 (1994), Powell, J. dissenting.

34 Pub.L. No. 104-132, 110 Stat. 1214 (1996).

35 Quoted in *The Death Penalty in America*, Hugo Bedau ed., Oxford Univ. Press, NY, 1997, p244.

36 Barry Scheck, Peter Neufeld, Jim Dwyer, *Actual Innocence*, Doubleday, NY, p36-7.

37 Barry Scheck, Peter Neufeld, Jim Dwyer, *Actual Innocence*, Doubleday, NY, pxiii.

38 61-AUT *Law and Contemporary Problems*, 125, "The ABA's Proposed Moratorium on the Death Penalty."

CHAPTER 3

1 *Chicago Tribune*, Dec. 22, 1985, "A Mystery Solved Only to Resurface."

2 *Victims of Justice*, Thomas Frisbie and Randy Garrett, Avon Books, NY, 1998

p.42

3   *Chicago Tribune*, Jan 23, 1985, "Cousin Linked to Murder Suspect Described Girl's Kidnap."

4   Det. John Sam, interview, Sept 19, 2001.

5   *Victims of Justice*-51, Witness Dan Fowler, who met Cruz in jail, first said Cruz claimed he knew who committed the crime. After the lunch break, he testified that Cruz was at the scene. Hernandez's cousin, Jackie Estremera, also changed his testimony on his second appearance before the grand jury.

6   *Victims of Justice*-122.

7   Det. John Sam, interview, Sept 19, 2001.

8   Tom Frisbee, reporter, *Chicago Sun-Times*, interview, Aug 25, 2000.

9   *Victims of Justice*-61.

10   *Chicago Tribune*, Dec 15, 1985, "Ex-Detective Says He Quit to Help Nicarico Defendants."

11   Tom Frisbee, *Chicago Sun-Times*, interview, Aug 25, 2000.

12   *Chicago Tribune*, Jan 31, 1985, "'Vision' Described in Girl's Slaying."

13   *Victims of Justice*-74.

14   *Chicago Tribune*, Jan 15, 1985, "Shoe Print Key to Murder Trial."

15   *Chicago Tribune*, Aug 31, 1995, "1 Pretrial Motion In the Cruz Travesty..." Eric Zorn.

16   *Chicago Tribune*, Feb 5, 1985, "Expert Links Boot to Girl's Slaying."

17   Det. John Sam, interview, Sept 19, 2001.

18   *Chicago Tribune*, Dec 15, 1985, "Ex-Detective Says He Quit to Help Nicarico Defendants."

19   *Victims of Justice*-91.

20   *Chicago Tribune*, Mar 16, 1985, "2 Get Death for Killing a Naperville Girl".

21   *Chicago Tribune*, Dec 17, 1985, "Ex-Prosecutor Denies Politics Outran Justice."

22   *Chicago Tribune*, Oct 18, 1995, "Dark Truths Buried in Nicarico Case May Yet See Light," Eric Zorn.

23   *Chicago Tribune*, Dec 12, 1985, "Melissa's Killer Clouds Pair's Death Row Case."

24   *Victims of Justice*-141.

25   *Victims of Justice*-141.

26   *Victims of Justice*-156.

27   *Chicago Tribune*, Mar 6, 1987, "Nicarico Death Suspect Freed."

28   *Chicago Tribune*, Jan 20, 1988, "Nicarico Convictions Reversed."

29   *Victims of Justice*-177.

30   Mary Brigid Kenney, interview, Sept 21, 2001

31   *Chicago Sun-Times*, Mar 6, 1992, "Burris Deputy Hits Nicarico Error."

32   Larry Marshall, interview, San Francisco, Nov. 2000.

33   *Chicago Tribune*, Oct 15, 1995, page 1.

34   *Victims of Justice*-255

35   *Chicago Tribune*, Oct 24, 1995, "Political Reputations on Line in Cruz Retrial".

36   *Chicago Tribune*, Oct 25, 1995, "Cruz Prosecutors Offer Case of Truth Stranger Than Fiction" Eric Zorn.

37   *Victims of Justice*-266.

38   Larry Marshall, interview, San Francisco, Nov 18, 2000.

39   *Victims of Justice*-237, 279.

40 *Chicago Tribune*, Jan 9, 1997, "It Appears Doing His Duty Has Cost Judge in Cruz Case."

41 William J. Kunkle Jr., Interview, Chicago, Aug 24, 2000.

CHAPTER 4

1   The founders of the People's Law Office included attorneys Dennis Cunningham and Skip Andrews who figured prominently in the Hampton case.

2   John Conroy, *Unspeakable Acts, Ordinary People*, Knopf, New York, 2000 p.69.

3   *Unspeakable Acts*, p.25.

4   *Unspeakable Acts*, p.159.

5   *Chicago Reader*, Jan 12, 1996, "Town Without Pity," John Conroy.

6   *The Chicago Reader*, "House of Screams," Jan 26, 1990, John Conroy.

7   *The Chicago Reader*, "The Shocking Truth," Jan 10, 1997, John Conroy.

8   *Unspeakable Acts*, 235.

9   *Chicago Tribune*, "Death Row Inmate Claims He Was Forced To Confess," Oct 4, 1998, Steve Mills.

10 *Chicago Sun-Times*, "The kids who saved Porter," Feb 21, 1999.

11 *Chicago Tribune*, "Death Row Inmate Guilt As Questionable As His Mental Fitness," Jan 28, 1999, Eric Zorn.

12 *Chicago Tribune*, Nov 17, 1999, "A Tortured Path to Death Row".

CHAPTER 5

1   *Chicago Tribune*, "Death Row Justice Derailed," Ken Armstrong and Steve Mills, Nov 14, 1999.

2   *Chicago Tribune*, "Victims, Heroes Travel Side By Side," Eric Zorn, Oct 27, 1998.

3   Ken Armstrong, interview, Sept 18, 2001.

4   *Chicago Tribune*, "Break Rules, Be Promoted," Ken Armstrong and Maurice Possley," Jan 14, 1999.

5   *Chicago Tribune*, "The Verdict: Dishonor," Ken Armstrong and Maurice Possley, Jan 10, 1999.

6   *Chicago Tribune*, "The Verdict: Dishonor," Ken Armstrong and Maurice Possley, Jan 10, 1999.

7   Ken Armstrong, interview, Sept 18, 2001.

8   *Chicago Tribune*, "Break Rules, Be Promoted," Ken Armstrong and Maurice Possley," Jan 14, 1999.

9   The state supreme court found that Scott had, among other things, allowed his key witness to lie under oath. See David Protess and Rob Warden, *A Promise of Justice*, Hyperion, NY, 1998, p.102.

10 *Chicago Tribune*, "Reversal of Fortune," Ken Armstrong and Maurice Possley," Jan 13, 1999.

11 *Chicago Tribune*, "Break Rules, Be Promoted," Ken Armstrong and Maurice Possley," Jan 14, 1999.

12 *Chicago Tribune*, "The Verdict: Dishonor," Ken Armstrong and Maurice Possley, Jan 10, 1999.

13 *Chicago Tribune*, "In the Wake of Pressure After Anthony Porter's Release..."

Feb 11, 1999.

14 *Chicago Tribune*, "500 Rally Against Executions," Mar 4, 1999.

15 *Chicago Tribune*, "Lawyers Press Ryan..." Mar 11, 1999.

16 *Chicago Tribune*, "Death Row Justice Derailed," Ken Armstrong and Steve Mills, Nov 14, 1999

17 "*Chicago Tribune*, "Yet Another Death Row Inmate Cleared," Steve Mills and Ken Armstrong, May 18, 1999.

18 Steve Mills, interview, Sept 18, 2001.

19 *Houston Chronicle*, "A deadly distinction: Part III," Feb 6, 2001.

CHAPTER 6

1 *Los Angeles Times*, July 3, 2001, "Justice O'Connor Doubts Fairness of Death Penalty," *AP*, Aug 2, 2001, "Court May Set Death Penalty Limits."

2 *Houston Chronicle*, "A Deadly Distinction, Part I," Feb 4, 2001.

3 An anonymous "Harris County, Texas, assistant district attorney," quoted by columnist Thom Marshall, *Houston Chronicle*, June 23, 2000.

4 Philadelphia Assistant District Attorney Jack McMahon, from a training tape published in "How to Pick a Jury," *Harpers*, July 2000.

5 "Win at All Costs - Government Misconduct in the Name of Expedient Justice," *Pittsburgh Post-Gazette*, A 10-part series beginning Nov 22, 1998.

6 Interview, Mike Farrell, Sherman Oaks, CA, January 5, 2000

7 "Deterrence, Brutalization, and the Death Penalty: Another Examination of Oklahoma's Return to the Death Penalty," William Bailey, 36 *Criminology* 711-33, 1998.

8 "Effects of Execution on Homicides in California," Ernie Thompson, 3 *Homicide Studies* p.129-150, 1997.

9 Raymond Bonner and Ford Fessenden,"States With No Death Penalty Share Lower Homicide Rates," *The New York Times*, Sept 22, 2000.

10 Michael L. Radelet and Ronald L. Akers, "Deterrence and the Death Penalty: The View of the Experts," *Journal of Criminal Law and Criminology* (Fall 1996), p14.11   Peter D. Hart Research Associates, 1995, quoted in Michael L. Radelet and Ronald L. Akers, "Deterrence and The Death Penalty: The View of the Experts," *Journal of Criminal Law and Criminology* (Fall 1996), p5.

11 "The High Cost of the Death Penalty to Taxpayers," David Erickson, California Death Penalty Focus.

13 *Palm Beach Post*, Jan 4, 2000.

14 Thomas Laquer, "Festival of Punishment," *London Review of Books*, Oct 5, 2000.

15 "A Deadly Distinction, Part I," *Houston Chronicle*, Feb 4, 2001.

16 *Savannah Morning News*, Jan 14, 2001.

17 Gallup Press Release, Feb 24, 2000; 66% of respondents favor the death penalty, down from 80 percent in 1994.

18 Charles Hoffman, Office of the Illinois State Appellate Defender, interview, Feb 1, 2000.

19 Steve Chapman, "Finding the Right Punishment for Murderers," *Chicago Tribune*, June 15, 2000.

20 *Houston Chronicle*, "A Deadly Distinction: Part IV," Feb 7, 2001.

21 *Weeks v. Angelone*, U.S. 99-5746, 2000.

22 "The Prison Odyssey of Sol Wachtler," *New York Times*, March 10, 1996.

23 "Another DNA Exoneration," *Washington Post*, Jan 26, 2001.

24 "Letting Go of McVeigh," *New York Times Magazine*, May 13, 2001.

25 "When He Speaks, They Listen," *Los Angeles Times*, Aug 21, 2001.

26 Suezann Bosler, "Legislators Refused to Hear Victims Against Death Penalty," *Tampa Tribune*, January 30, 2000.

27 "Europe's View of the Death Penalty," *New York Times*, editorial, May 13, 2001.

28 Rod Dreher, "Feds Shake Faith in Death Penalty," *New York Post*, May 15, 2001.

29 Jim Yardley, "Execution on TV Brings Little Solace," *New York Times*, June 11, 2001.

30 Michael L. Radelet, Hugo Adam Bedau, Constance E. Putnam, *In Spite of Innocence: Erroneous Convictions in Capital Cases*, Northeastern University Press, Boston, 1992.

31 *Coleman v. Thompson*, III S. Ct 2546, 1991; *The Boston Globe*, June 2, 2000, "Judge Denies Bid for DNA Test".

32 *Los Angeles Times*, July 22, 2001, "'92 Execution Haunts Death Penalty Foes".

33 *Los Angeles Times*, Aug 14, 2001, "Ruling on Sleeping Lawyer."

34 *AP*, Sept 10, 2001, "Suspended Police Chemist Awaits Fate;" *AP*, Sept 25, 2001, "Embattled Police Chemist fired;" *National Catholic Reporter*, July 27, 2001, "Oklahoma Governor Reconsiders Death Penalty."

35 *Journal of Criminal Law and Criminology* (Fall 1996), Michael Radelet and Ronald Akers, "Deterrence and the Death Penalty: The View of the Experts," p14: Present and former presidents of the most prestigious criminological societies, polled in 1995, overwhelmingly said they did not think the death penalty significantly reduces the homicide rate (94 percent), and they knew of no empirical evidence that would support such a claim (94.1 percent).

36 See notes 10 and 11 above.

37 *Chicago Tribune*, Mar 4, 1999, "500 Rally Against Executions."

Index

photo: Carol Gray

About the Author

After a distinguished career as a documentary filmmaker—
American Revolution II, The Murder of Fred Hampton—Mike
Gray drew on his engineering background to craft the original
screenplay for the eerily prescient film, The China Syndrome.
He continues to write for film and television, and his recent
book, *Drug Crazy*, helped fuel the current national debate on
drug policy. Mr. Gray lives in Los Angeles.